Where the Waters Part

1/10/2020

To my good friend
Richard Rodgers MD .

Many thanks for your
encouragement in this project.

JTW

An early American water mill

Where the Waters Part

A Family's Search for Freedom and Authenticity:
Nine Generations of Wards, Early Settlers of
Augusta County, Virginia, and Their Descendants

James F. Ward Jr.

RESOURCE *Publications* • Eugene, Oregon

WHERE THE WATERS PART
A Family's Search for Freedom and Authenticity: Nine Generations of
Wards, Early Settlers of Augusta County, Virginia, and Their Descendants

Resource Publications
An Imprint of Wipf and Stock Publishers
199 W. 8th Ave., Suite 3
Eugene, OR 97401

www.wipfandstock.com

PAPERBACK ISBN: 978-1-5326-9631-2
HARDCOVER ISBN: 978-1-5326-9632-9
EBOOK ISBN: 978-1-5326-9633-6

Manufactured in the U.S.A.   NOVEMBER 21, 2019

For my grandchildren:

Abigail

Emma

Caitlyn

Benjamin

Bethany

And God said, Let there be a firmament in the midst of the waters, and let it divide the waters from the waters. And God made the firmament, and divided the waters which were under the firmament from the waters which were above the firmament: and it was so. And God called the firmament Heaven.

—Genesis 1:6–8a

Contents

List of Illustrations

Preface

WHEN I BEGAN TO explore the Ward family history, no account of my family line existed, and it seemed that someone, presumably a family member, should step forward and write one, at least for the benefit of future generations. I considered whether I should be the one to carry out such a project, that is, if I could do it justice. I did not see that the end result would amount to more than a set of notes about the family going back more than a generation or two. I thought these notes could prove useful when I would tell family stories to my grandchildren.

Then it occurred to me to expand the project's scope to include a bit of material from generations before my grandparents. To do so, I could add, here and there, a few interesting stories from their lives. But as I proceeded, I saw that genealogical research and writing could be an enjoyable activity in itself, something like working on a jigsaw puzzle: fitting many pieces together to reveal a larger picture. It also satisfied my growing curiosity about my forebears.

These were my original motivations for writing, but I began to see they were not primary. I found that, ultimately, I was after more than a set of notes. I had questions about these people whose answers could, perhaps, reveal something about myself as well: What were these Wards like as individuals and together, as family? What, if anything, was distinctive about them? What was driving them toward what ends? I wondered, could this project provide answers?

As I began to write up the material I found, some of the old family stories came back into my mind, many of them stories of events in which I had been a participant or observer. Others were reconstructed, with a bit of imagination, from old photos or scribbled notes in the front of books that someone-or-other had given me. I also remembered that some of the stories had been repeated *ad infinitum* by the old-timers, often really just fragments of stories, seemingly of small importance for the larger story I was trying to tell. Yet they could not easily be put out of mind.

My involvement with the project changed considerably after I retired in 2015. Now I had more time to "surf the Web," to explore haphazardly, and in the process learn more of the names and events of the family and perhaps, with a bit of luck, finding meaningful connections. I did this just to see what new material might come to light. My curiosity and interest started to build, especially when I found a few savory nuggets—tasty tidbits of information suggestive of what was really going on with this family. I got more serious about the research process and about learning the truth. I joined the Seattle Genealogical Society, and I made regular appearances on the ninth floor of the Central Branch of the Seattle Public Library (the location of its genealogical collection).

I soon realized that, depending on the perspective of the narrator, there were *many* possible true stories that could be written about this family. I was seeking *one* that would reveal this family's distinctive, authentic personality, if indeed it could be said to have one. It seemed that my writing objective was to produce a narrative grounded in history: a compelling and truthful story faithful to the historical details and revealing of character. The story of the family as a whole would have to be built up from the stories of its individual members into a coherent structure shaped by an overarching theme, again assuming that an overarching theme was discoverable and could be named. That theme would give this family's story continuity and credibility over a time span of 250 years. That, at least, was my intention. But as it turned out, more than one such overarching theme emerged.

One that seemed promising was migration. The theme of migration tied together three major geographic relocations over the nine generations. They were journeys (1) across the Atlantic Ocean from the north of Ireland to Philadelphia, then into the western frontier of Pennsylvania and the Mid-Atlantic region (southwestern Virginia); (2) from the Mid-Atlantic to the Deep South (Georgia and Alabama); and (3) from the Deep South to the Southwest (Texas), then on to the West Coast (California) and points beyond. Together they would provide a time-and-space map for exploring this family's motives and intentions as they undertook these travel adventures. Migration would become an overarching theme for telling their story. I wondered if the relocations were motivated by a wish to break away *from* something, to reach out *for* something, or perhaps to greet their destiny in an engagement *with* the unknown.

Putting the latter concerns temporarily to the side, I found, from an examination of time lines, that I could identify younger family members throughout the generations who must have been present at family gatherings (let's say, family gatherings by the fireside after dinner) when tales of adventure, hardship, courage, victory, humor, or entertainment were shared. By "tales" I mean stories that were *true*, not fabricated, though they may have been embellished for storytelling effect. These stories would have been recounted by the participants, eyewitnesses, or others with an inside knowledge of events—stories that would then be repeated over and over to the next generation, then to the generation after that, and so on down the line in an oral tradition. The tales would be told with "authenticity," that is, with power to convey a set of character ideals to the youngsters.

I thought that perhaps those stories (if I could bring the crucial ones into the light) might hold the key to how I wanted to understand our family, learn the truth of its values, discover its particularities and its oddities, and provide a way to memorialize them to my descendants. What I have tried to do in this book is recover (or probably better said, reconstruct) what I remember, or might have remembered, from stories, had I heard them directly from family storytellers across the generations. Many of them came from my own memory, either from my direct experience of events or from hearing a story, perhaps many times, from a cousin or other family member still alive (or still alive in my memory). Others came from printed or recorded sources to which I had access.

I have become convinced that those stories contain not just the memories of individual people, but the collective memory carried by them (or rather, by us), full of clues to the kind of people they were: their personalities; values; and reasons for their actions, agendas, and motives.[1] They could partly explain why I am the way I am and why we, the Ward family, ended up the way we did. Memory, I think, is more than the content of an individual's consciousness at a given moment; it includes what lies below the surface of the mind, what is unconsciously preserved there, and what may potentially be brought up into awareness for reflection and understanding. And, arguably, it includes what lies within the reach of group recollection, including what lies within historical material, either transmitted orally or stored in printed or electronic form.

So this work takes the form of an essay on my (and our family's) recovery of memory, aided by genealogical resources and historical research with material from still-living family members, including myself. My hope is that it may prove interesting, useful, or even inspirational to present and future generations of our family, and potentially to others, as they consider what it means to live "freely and authentically" according to the Wards.

---

1. "Freud regarded memory and motive as inseparable. Recollection could have no force, no meaning, unless it was allied with motive," in Sacks, *Consciousness*, 96.

Acknowledgments

THANKS ARE DUE TO my wife, Elizabeth, for being a patient listener as I recounted many family stories and for offering many helpful suggestions and editorial assistance. Also, I want to thank my son, David, for his research assistance in travels to Ireland, Georgia, Virginia, and Texas.

Two of my Texas cousins, Julia Nelle Vandine and Sharon Ward Blancarte, generously offered family stories and other material that enriched the book. My sisters Marion Ward Morford and Susan Ward Adams provided perspective for the life of James F. Ward Sr.

Thanks are also due to Traci West, Special Collections Librarian at Dallas Baptist University, who provided archival material for the chapter on Jesse Lawrence Ward.

Key Figures of This Story and Their Spouses by Generation

1. James Ward "the Elder" (1672–1758) / Sarah Rodgers (1685–1730)
2. John Ward (1704–1786) / Mary A. Campbell (1705–1743)
3. Jacob Ward (1730–1791) / Virginia A. Hill (1730–1791)
4. William Ward (1757–1850) / Sarah Vernon (1764–1840)
5. Abner V. Ward (1787–1837) / Frances J. Kidd (1790–1848)
6. Lawrence L. Ward (1829–1895) / Lucy A. Marshall (1835–1919)
7. William E. Ward (1861–1893) / Tabitha C. Paschall (1865–1893); Jesse L. Ward, DD (1866–1952) / 1. Jennie Beard (1866–1907), 2. Elizabeth Penn Dickson (1879–1965)
8. Julian E. Ward Sr. (1885–1950) / Henrietta E. Brothers (1890–1983)
9. James F. Ward Sr., MD (1912–1988) / Rubye K. Hutchings (1921–2007); H. Winnelle Ward (1915–1989) / William H. Nelle, PhD (1911–1998); Julian E. Ward Jr., MD (1927–1962) / Alma A. Kreider (1925–1991)

Nine Generations of Wards

(Abridged)

James Ward "the Elder"
(1672–1758)

James Ward II
(1700–1763)

William Ward
(1702–1765)

John Ward
(1704–1786)

Isaac Ward
(1708–?)

Cpt James Ward III
(1727–1774)

William Ward
(1725–1795)

David Ward
(1740–1827)

John Ward Jr.
(1727–1787)

Jacob Ward
(1730–1791)

Elizabeth Ward Delong
(1743–1818)

Col William Ward
(1752–1822)

Cpt James Ward IV
(1763–1846)

John Ward "White Wolf"
(1754–1793)

John Ward
(1755–1838)

Sgt William Ward
(1757–1850)

Jacob Ward Jr.
(1761–1827)

Abner Ward
(1787–1837)

Lawrence Lafayette Ward
(1829–1895)

Henry L. Ward
(1854–1934)

William E. Ward
(1861–1893)

James Francis Ward
(1863–1920)

Jesse L. Ward, DD (hon)
(1866–1952)

William E. Ward
(1861–1893)

James Francis Ward
(1863–1920)

Julian E. Ward Sr
(1885–1950)

James Franklin Ward Sr MD
(1912–1988)

H. Winnelle Ward Nelle
(1915–1989)

Maj Julian E. Ward Jr MD
(1927–1962)

Introduction

THIS IS A STORY of the Wards, a family descended from Scotch-Irish settlers living in colonial-era Augusta County, Virginia, a family of English heritage with roots in the north of Ireland. It follows nine generations over a period of 250 years, beginning with the Irish immigrants James Ward "the Elder" (fifty-eight-year-old widower) and his immediate family members: sons James II (with his wife and children), William, and John.[1]

About 1730, they sailed west from the most northerly part of Ireland—the Inishowen Peninsula in County Donegal, Ulster—across the Atlantic to Philadelphia. They settled down for a few years in Scotch-Irish communities in Chester and Cumberland Counties, Pennsylvania, and then, moving south and west with the flow of immigrants traveling on the Great Wagon Road, eventually arrived in the backcountry of southwestern Virginia at different times during the late 1740s or early 1750s.

John Ward, second in the line of Wards who are the focus of this account (see Key Figures of This Story), was the first member of the family to make his way into Augusta County in 1744, going into Virginia as the family's trail blazer ahead of the father and brothers, who stayed behind in Pennsylvania for a few more years.

Four generations of these Wards lived in Virginia, the last being that of John's grandson, (Sergeant) William Ward, a Revolutionary War soldier. After the war, in 1786, William brought his

---

1. Some accounts include another son, Isaac.

wife and young family south from Culpeper County, Virginia to Elbert County, Georgia.

Two generations later, in 1850, William's grandson Lawrence Lafayette "L. L." Ward headed west to Upshur County in East Texas, traveling with his young wife, Lucy, and her parents and several of her siblings. In 1858, just seven years after that migration, L. L. and Lucy moved even farther west to Wise County in North Texas. Three more generations of Wards would eventually call Texas home.

Members of the last generation of Texans (all of whom I knew personally) grew up in Wichita Falls in Wichita County and in Lubbock in West Texas, where the family settled in the 1930s and 40s, during the difficult years of the Great Depression and World War II. They pursued their dreams—or fought their demons—in various parts of the western United States: Texas, California, Washington, and Wyoming. Yet they managed to stay connected with one another.

This last generation comprises the three children of my paternal grandparents, Julian E. Ward Sr. and Henrietta Brothers: James F. Ward Sr., MD, World War II veteran and ophthalmologist; Winnelle Ward Nelle, social worker and property manager; and Major Julian E. Ward Jr., MD, Air Force flight surgeon and pioneer of the US space program.

In undertaking to write the story of the Wards, I am indebted to John F. Campbell, the author of *The Campbells of Drumaboden* (1925). His work was helpful to me because John Ward married into the Campbell family of Drumaboden, Kilmacrenan, County Donegal about the time he came to America. *The Campbells* describes the political and religious ideals held by this prominent family of Scotch-Irish Presbyterians as they made their way into the American South. The book deals primarily with the branch of the Campbell family that emigrated from Ireland to Franklin in Williamson County, Tennessee prior to the Civil War. However, another branch of the same family, the one which the present story of Wards concerns, migrated to Augusta County much earlier than that (viz., during the 1720s), and ahead of the Wards. The

Campbells became the Wards' in-laws through John's marriage to Mary Ann Campbell (about 1726).

The Campbells was published nearly a century ago. It is an example of a family history told in the setting of Scottish, Irish, and United States history, providing contextual information that helps understand the Campbell family. In telling their story, the author shows how the Campbells were formed by their commitments to community, to religion, and to politics; these commitments became a part of the Wards' heritage.

The present work similarly tells the Ward family story in historical context. Furthermore, I tell it from a certain point of view: the Wards' search for freedom and authenticity over nine generations. Although it is *a* story, it is not *the* story. It is merely *one* story among many others that could be told.

By saying it is a story of a search for freedom and authenticity, I am describing how I see this family move along a trajectory of time and space, along a path of personal and social transformation, toward their destiny: a distinctive way of flourishing in America.

As I reflect on the various family members' lives and experiences, I see common patterns in the way they would go about the daily business of living their lives while being influenced by potent memories from the past, memories that had the power to shape them and make claims upon them. These were memories of ethical ideals, ideals of being and becoming human that they believed essential, or good and right, for their self-fulfillment. Ethical ideals defined what it meant for them to be free and authentic.

Foremost of the Wards' ideals was *faithfulness to oneself*—being faithful to who or what one really is. In other words, it meant *being true to one's character, maintaining one's self-respect*. While this ideal mostly revealed itself as something positive, as a strength of character, it could also emerge as an overly high opinion of oneself, in stubbornness, or in being easily offended.

Faithfulness to oneself was distinct from, but closely related to, another ideal: *protecting (or enhancing) one's reputation*. Again, this ideal was mostly positive, but it might have negative sides, such as being overly concerned with public appearance or presentation, projecting an outward image in conflict with one's character, or needing to be right in disagreements with others.

A corollary to the ideals of self-respect and reputation was that of *truthfulness*: acting and speaking consistently with the facts, as one understood them, in order to be single-minded—a person of integrity. If contrary facts should emerge or one is *wrong* (not just proven wrong in the court of public opinion), then one should be willing to make appropriate admissions, corrections, and amendments to preserve a commitment to truth, even if, in taking those actions, there could be a short-term cost to one's self-image.

We might say, in today's psychologically oriented language, that remembering and striving to live by a set of ethical ideals, valued over time by one's own kith and kin, defines what it means to be an "authentic person" or to embrace an "authentic self." Remembering those ideals and striving to live life ordered by them—living authentically—is the essence of a *successful* life. Living authentically means true self-fulfillment. It means, essentially, that one is on the right path in life. It does not mean that one is self-centered. Nor does it mean that one has already arrived and achieved perfection. It means one is guided by a sense of self that is larger than an "individualist self" which devalues relationships and sees others as means, not ends. [2]

Besides desiring authenticity, the Wards also sought freedom, like so many new arrivals in America, even being willing, if necessary, to detach themselves from some of their historical commitments (which might include social, political, or religious traditions) to achieve what was possible given the opportunities before them. Their goals were achieved by sheer strength of determination, grit, and native intelligence. They certainly did not question their strength of determination ("willpower"), intelligence, or ability to persuade others to join their cause. This conceit sometimes appeared as an unusual sales ability or ability to make friends (or enemies).

2. For a longer discussion of the way I am using the terms "authenticity" and "self," see Taylor, *Ethics* and *Sources*.

The search for freedom, on the other hand, might reduce to a stereotypically American, individualistic, self-centered ethic of "lifestyle choice."[3] Although lifestyle choice is, these days, a common way to speak of personal freedom that suggests a kind of self-fulfillment, more must be said than how they made their choices in order to adequately describe the kind of people these Wards were. That is why I also mentioned authenticity—true self-fulfillment in living lives shaped by the themes and ethical ideals which truly fulfilled them—alongside freedom to pursue what might appeal to the passions of the moment.

My aim is to understand—or perhaps better said, *creatively infer*—the motivations behind the choices they made or rejected and the traditions they followed or left behind, based on the historical data available. Understanding their motives goes a long way toward understanding who these people were and what they were like in their social interactions. I acknowledge the speculative nature of assigning motives to people unavailable to speak for themselves. Nevertheless, my inferences are grounded in the story of real people who really lived in a particular time and place. I have no doubt that the future will see revisions to the data, and alternative inferences will be proposed by others on the basis of those revisions. I expect that to happen and welcome it.

An insight into the Wards' motivations may be gained by considering their occupational choices. Besides employment as farm workers or small business owners such as carpenters or mill operators, many of them became guardians or peacekeepers of one kind or another: militiamen, soldiers, sheriffs, or justices of the peace. Interestingly, the occupational theme of guardian is consistent with the medieval origin of the English name Ward, derived from the French "de la Varde," which means, literally, "of the guard." According to one ancestral account, our family's distant ancestor, Richard de la Varde (born about 1040), is said to have been William the Conqueror's "noble captain of the guard."[4]

---

3. For a longer discussion of American "individualism" and "lifestyles," see Bellah et al., *Habits*.

4. Ebert, "Richard de la Warde".

Another occupational theme arises from the Wards' emergence as community leaders, educators, healers or explorers as seen in their professional roles of ministers, doctors, teachers, administrators, or scientists. A streak of moral idealism is on display in all these occupations, appearing as *a desire to understand a complex situation, explain, enlighten, protect or improve the situation by helping others.* That is, in these roles they upheld the guardian/peacekeeper ideal, guided by strong convictions about the truth of things, at the same time following their natural curiosity by investigating the unknown. The unknown might be truth about God, humanity, or the natural world. In short, they were *guided by moral convictions* that they also wanted to pass on to their family members or share with others in the community. These convictions should be considered distinct from, and more basic than, a commitment to a conventional morality, whether of a social, political, or religious nature.

Pursuit of freedom and authenticity together may have motivated some of the Wards to boldly break with the traditions that had been their heritage, leading to better, or perhaps worse, consequences. They may have thought they had received permission, by reason of their idealism, creativity, or convictions, to follow a new way, breaking with an older tradition that seemed no longer relevant. That new tradition, or new light thrown on an existing tradition, might result in a change in religious, communal, or political affiliation, or perhaps in a change of occupation or physical proximity to friends and relatives. It might also lead to some kind of erratic or eccentric behavior, "marching to the tune of a different drummer," or to exhibiting non-conventional thinking. Decisions and actions like these might well apply to the new directions taken by family pioneers and leaders.

The family story that I want to tell has, as its backdrop, events in the history of the British Isles, Ireland, and America, including the Scotch-Irish wave of migration from Ireland to North America (1718–1736), the American Revolutionary War (1775–1783), the American Civil War (1861–1865), the Great Depression

(1929–1939), World War II (1939–1945), and the Space Race era of the US-USSR Cold War (1957–1969).

Besides these better-known historical periods, I want to take note of other, lesser-known periods that are relevant to this story, including the First Great Awakening in colonial Virginia (1755–1775), a consequence of which was the rise of the (Separate) Baptists in Virginia (1769–1775) prior to the Revolutionary War; the legislative initiatives in Virginia, following the War, that affected the separation of church and state within the United States; and the status of Texas in the decade prior to the Civil War (1851–1861).

Religious history, in particular, is important to the Ward story because Presbyterians, Baptists, and other dissenting religious groups, with whom family members were at various times associated, exhibited an attractive set of ideals to support the Wards' understanding of a free life well lived. For instance, if one were to break with one's particular religious tradition, that did not mean, necessarily, that one also broke with all of the ideals of that tradition, or that one accepted all the ideals espoused by some alternative religious tradition or philosophical perspective. There was both change and continuity across the traditions variously claiming the Wards' allegiance.

Religious history is important for political reasons, too, because religious groups participated in crucial church-state conversations with people like James Madison and Thomas Jefferson prior to Virginia's ratification of the Constitution of the United States and its First Amendment. These documents helped determine the meaning of "freedom" in America. We know from written evidence that at least one Ward family member, Jacob Ward, engaged in these conversations.

The story told here also reveals some of the negative consequences of this particular family's exercise of its free will, a freedom that could sometimes be exhibited in stubborn, egotistical, self-centered ambition, or in restlessness, over-competitiveness and, at least in a couple of instances, in lives going "off the rails" into social impropriety. It focuses primarily, but not exclusively, on the stories of the male family members in this line because, so far at least, the male names have been linked to more of the available historical and genealogical information on which I heavily depended.

To restate, I have no doubt that the future will see many erroneous historical or genealogical details corrected or supplemented by new information. I am neither a historian nor a genealogist by training, only a mathematician. By training and habit, I tend to look for patterns in incomplete data and try to "connect the dots" and validate the patterns with more data when possible. I do not claim this present effort to be a scientific exercise. Historical truth does not lie in formal validation of the conclusions. Conclusions are always provisional, subject to further revision. I hope the results will prove both interesting and plausible. And only the reader can judge its success in that regard.

To my readers, please consider this an invitation to discover what may be lacking or inaccurate in the present account and write your own story, consistent with the data. I accept responsibility for all limitations, especially for the all-too-brief treatment of the exceptional women who have kept the men of the family, for the most part, on the right path, women sometimes laboring under difficult or even scandalous circumstances. Examples of long-suffering women who deserve a fuller account include Frances Julia Kidd (wife of Abner Vernon Ward), Lucy Ann Marshall (wife of Lawrence Lafayette Ward), Henrietta E. Brothers (wife of Julian Elvis Ward Sr.), and Rubye Katherine Hutchings (wife of James F. Ward Sr.).

I note that three generations of the Ward family were slave owners, more accurately known as slave holders or enslavers. This fact I cannot and would not attempt to justify. It does not, of course, square with the slave owners' searches for freedom and authenticity *for themselves*. I should also note, however, that after my investigation of L. L. Ward's early life in Alabama, his 1851 migration to Texas, and his subsequent life in Deep Creek, I could find no record of him ever being a slave owner. Apparently, he broke with the slave-owning tradition of the Wards, which extended back three previous generations, from Jacob and William to Abner. (L. L.'s in-laws, the Marshalls, were also slave owners, and may have brought slaves with them to East Texas during their migration there with their daughter and son-in-law.) L. L. Ward would seem to have departed from the Wards' slave-holding tradition at least a decade before the Civil War broke out.

As indicated earlier, this story has two overarching narratives, at times in tension, narratives that display the family's character through the set of ideals they valued and consciously or unconsciously exhibited over the generations: 1) searching for *freedom* in both the positive sense (freedom to pursue a goal) and the negative sense (freedom to break down a barrier) in order to explore new paths, circumstances, or opportunities; and 2) seeking *authenticity*, remembering and striving to live up to their ethical ideals. Besides those mentioned previously, they included improving the material, educational, and social circumstances of family members or of the community, working with intelligence and persistence, and being a moral exemplar.

Beyond my interest in this subject as a Ward family member and as a family storyteller, I would like to share this account more widely because, first, I think a perspective from history helps us all make greater sense of our lives. We live in a time in America that is chaotic and confusing—to put it mildly—a fact that is painfully obvious to everyone alive at this moment late in the second decade of the 21st century. These days, truth and morality are widely viewed as untethered from tradition, matters of an individual's "free choice" or a narrow sense of "facts." But truly, we have inherited the values and attitudes of earlier generations for better or worse (but I think mostly for the better), and many of these challenge the present-day ethos of radical individualism or tribalism. The earlier generations may actually be able to guide us in our pursuit of freedom and authenticity (even if we are not clear that's what we are searching for) so that we might understand what counts as success or failure and be able to choose our actions wisely.

Second, the story may help to preserve a memory of success by a poor Scotch-Irish immigrant family that, for the most part, did good as it did well in America. I think this achievement was a consequence of the ideals these Wards carried with them across the Atlantic into America and over the generations. They did live authentically, for the most part. And we, the Ward family of today, have received much from them. Theirs was not a stereotypical story of "rags to riches," but rather, a story of hard-scrabble life entering the American middle-class, where, in the case of this family, the middle-class success lay in the creation of social capital, or social well-being, and not so much in the creation of material wealth. And I think that achievement is worth memorializing.

Third, the story preserves some aspects of the Scotch-Irish experience in America that may not be as widely known and appreciated as that of other ethnic groups, partly because these people were aware from the beginning that they had a vital stake in being known simply as "Americans" and therefore did not go to any great lengths to preserve their distinctive history, which they did not see as exceptional; in this belief they were too modest.

1

Beginnings in Britain, Ireland and America

IF WE ACCEPT AS fact, as some genealogists have, that this family found its way into Britain from Normandy with Duke William in 1066, and take as historically verified that the Normans trace their ancestry to the Vikings, then we can say that this Ward family is descended from the Vikings.[1],[2] An account of Wards from the English Yorkshire region near the Scottish borderlands claims as their ancestor a certain Richard de la Varde, born about 1040, arriving in England with William the Conqueror, Duke of Normandy, in 1066.

Another account names a William de la Ward as an early English resident of the post-Norman era:

> Seven hundred and ten distinguished persons, each bearing but one name, accompanied William, the Conqueror, from Normandy to the conquest of England in 1066; a record of all of whose names is yet preserved. Among the number, was 'Ward, one of the noble Captains.' This is

1. Collins, "Richard de la Warde."
2. C. Ward, "Ancient History."

the earliest period in which the name is found in English history, and the first which appears there with an additional [first] name was William de la Ward, residing in Chester, in 1175.[3]

However the Wards came into England or Scotland, it is also claimed that they first appeared in Ireland in the Inishowen Peninsula, County Donegal, during or shortly after King James's Ulster Plantation of 1609.[4] That would make sense if, according to the king's plan for control of the population in northern Ireland, they were identifiable as belonging to some variety of Protestant non-conformist group sent to Ulster to quell the Catholic native Irish uprisings. They would then have been living in Ireland through the time of the "Glorious" Revolution of 1688, concluded by the Siege of Derry (1688–1689) and defeat of James II by the forces of William of Orange. Although the immediate danger from the native Catholics would have abated, the peace that followed would have meant a difficult forty years of the Wards living as tenants of absentee English landlords. That situation could have provided a good reason for them to leave Ireland and make a new life in America.

Consider the case of Ward neighbor John Lewis. One of the leaders of the Scotch-Irish influx into America, John Lewis (1678–1762), an emigrant from the same area of Donegal as James Ward the Elder and six years his junior, was forced to flee Ireland in 1728 (two years before the Wards left) after a shoot-out in which his landlord attempted to evict him, in the process wounding Lewis's wife and killing his brother as he lay in a sickbed; in the return fire the landlord was killed. Lewis was charged with murder. Although he was eventually acquitted of the charge, the acquittal occurred only after he had fled the country, first to Portugal, then to Virginia.

Lewis's case, like that of many other of their Ulster neighbors, is relevant to the Wards' situation. The numbers of the Scotch-Irish and reasons for their leaving Ireland about this time have been

3. A. Ward, *Ward Family*, vi.

4. Cooper, "John Ward" identifies this immigrant from England as "Reverend John Ward." He is presumed elsewhere to be a Puritan reverend.

considered elsewhere. Dickson[5] estimates that fifteen thousand Irish emigrants entered the American colonies during 1721–1730, most of whom were Protestants from the north of Ireland. Most of those Protestants were Scotch-Irish Presbyterians. Reasons (perhaps excuses) for their emigration given by an observer at the time (1729)[6] included

1. Opportunity for a better economic life for the children of the emigrants,

2. Discontent with landlords for raising rents unreasonably and with the (Anglican) clergy for extracting tithes,

3. Oppression of the dissenting Presbyterians,

4. Favorable employment opportunities believed to exist for immigrants coming to America, and

5. Improved social standing for women.

Dickson found that religion was a lesser consideration; resentment against landlords for arbitrarily and unreasonably raising rents ("rack-renting") and anger for having to pay tithes to support a state church were the most compelling reasons for emigration. It was the *unfairness* of having to pay the required tithes that was especially galling to the dissenters; they had to support their own clergy in addition to supporting the Anglican clergy.

From these considerations, we might plausibly believe that 1, 2, and 4 were the main reasons the Wards came to America, seeking new opportunities for themselves and their children (a positive freedom) and seeking to escape from oppression by landlords and clergy (a negative freedom). The first and fourth reasons may be inferred from the fact that these people were poor and three generations of the Ward family left Ireland together, and the second may be inferred from widespread discontent with the state and landlords, as seen in the Lewis case. I found no evidence that reasons 3 or 5 played a role, but they remain possibilities.

5. Dickson, "Religion," chapter 3 in Dickson, *Ulster*, 1721-30.

6. Stewart, "Letter." This letter was written near the peak of the Scotch-Irish emigration to America. (Judge Michael Ward was not related to our Wards.)

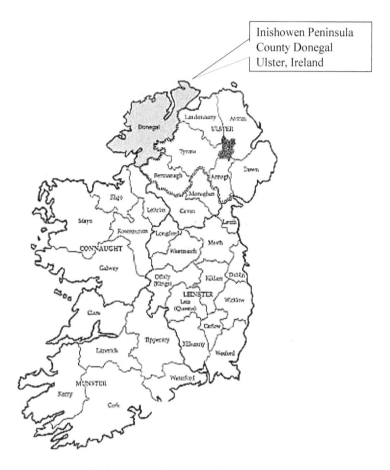

Inishowen Peninsula
County Donegal
Ulster, Ireland

Figure 1. Ireland, showing the location of the Inishowen Peninsula in County Donegal

John Lewis and his partners, William Beverly and James Patton, were important figures in the Virginia immigration of the 1720s and 30s, since together they paved the way for large numbers of the Scotch-Irish—most of whom initially settled in Pennsylvania—to find inexpensive land and put down roots in Augusta County. When the Scotch-Irish moved from point A to point B, they moved in a coordinated fashion. That pattern was distinctive of the emigrants, according to Hannah and Hannah:

In those days people often emigrated in groups. Sometimes it would be a family or a group of neighbors. In a few cases the entire congregation of a church emigrated together. Sometimes a single family member would go first and find a place to settle in the new land, then other members of his family—brothers, uncles, and cousins, and perhaps neighbors—would join him. The Scotch-Irish were no exception to this pattern.[7]

This pattern of emigration was true for the Wards as they joined family, friends, and neighbors in making the dangerous and expensive voyage to America. They sought freedom from the harsh conditions in Ireland and freedom to find economic opportunity in the New Country.

7. Hannah et al., "People," 9.

2

Pennsylvania:
The Great Wagon Road

JOHN WARD WAS THE third youngest of three, or possibly four, brothers, sons of James Ward "the Elder" and Sarah Rodgers, who came to America with their widowed father from the northern part of Ireland about 1730. John was born in the Inishowen Peninsula, County Donegal, in 1704; his father and older brothers, James and William, were also born there, in 1672, 1700, and 1702, respectively. A younger brother, Isaac (born in 1708?), may have come with them. According to ship's passenger records, John sailed for America in 1728 as an indentured servant.

His indentured servant record was filed at St. Sepulcher's, London in July 1728, at which time John was described as single, age twenty-four, a carpenter bound for Maryland with a four-year term of service.[1] This arrangement would have provided him with money to pay for ship's passage to America, establish him in a trade, and possibly allow him to acquire land there as well. Indentured service was not slavery but voluntary servitude under the terms of a mutually agreeable contract. It was a very common

1. Kaminkow et al., *List*, 292.

way to secure passage and the beginnings of a new life in America, without stigma attached.

While this record indicates that John was voluntarily entering servitude as a single person, we have reason to think that at this time he had a wife and (at least) one young child. That wife was Mary Ann Campbell, daughter of the prominent Campbell family of Drumaboden, Kilmacrenan, County Donegal, Ulster, Ireland. The Campbells were staunch Presbyterians, originally from Argyll, Scotland.

A traditional family story says that when John left Ireland, he had one son. Later, when his wife arrived in America, he found that another son had been born after he left. So it may be that by 1730 he had two sons (with a daughter born a few years later).

Passenger records also show that John's brother William, two years his senior, arrived by the following year in Rappahannock County, Virginia. He was also an indentured servant and unmarried at age twenty-seven.[2] (William would marry a Jane Swain in Philadelphia in 1737; he and the other Wards would eventually find their way from Pennsylvania into Augusta County, Virginia, sometime after John arrived there in 1744.)

William, like John, may also have arrived in America with practical skills, such as those of a stonemason or carpenter, skills that could be put to immediate use. I infer this from a county record from 1761 stating that the Augusta County Parish entered into an agreement with William Ward and William Preston to build a parsonage using building materials taken from the land, meaning that it was to be built by them from timber and/or stone, for the price of £300.[3]

James II, the oldest of the brothers, was already married when he arrived in America in 1730 at age thirty. He traveled from Ireland with his immediate family: widowed father James Ward "the Elder," age fifty-eight; wife Ann Chiles Ward, twenty-five; and sons William and James III, ages five and three, respectively. Although this family was by no means impoverished, they would have had to

2. Coldham, *King's*, 40.
3. Chalkley, *Chronicles*, 2:494-95.

carefully plan their finances for the trip to America, including initial living expenses. Pooling resources, the elder and the younger James would have had the money to pay for the family's passage, without the need for James to enter into indentured service like his brothers John and William.

Indications are that John and William traveled to America separately from James II and his immediate family, but this fact is not entirely clear from passenger records. They were both young, single, and readily employable, equipped with skills much in demand in the colonies.[4] (In other words, they could fend for themselves, and they might even be able to help the other family members get established in America.)

It appears that in arriving before the other family members, John had been entrusted to be their pathfinder, charged with finding a suitable place for them to live in the new country and reliable passage to it. In regard to this responsibility, he was apparently successful, and that success was partly due to the fact that he was not proceeding blindly or moving completely into the unknown. He was finding a path across the Atlantic Ocean and through the American backcountry, which had been previously marked out by a great many people immigrating from the north of Ireland into Pennsylvania. Their numbers were especially great during the years of peak immigration of the Scotch-Irish, 1714–1736.

As it turned out, John found welcoming Scotch-Irish friends in East Caln Township, Chester County, Pennsylvania (near present-day Downingtown, a few miles west of Philadelphia). Of particular note, one of their neighbors there—one that John already knew from back home in Ireland—was James Lockhart, a contemporary of John's father, who had earlier come to East Caln Township with his family, traveling from the Irish town of Soppoq, Templemore (known today as Muff, located just north of Derry) in County Donegal. The Lockhart family made the trip to America about ten years before the Wards. They surely would have

---

4. Although some sources say these brothers traveled to America with James "the Elder" and others in the family, I have not been able to verify this.

sent back reports about America to the Wards in Ireland, probably encouraging them to join them in East Caln.

The Ward and Lockhart families were not merely neighbors; they were close friends. In 1730, the younger James Ward and Lockhart's son Jacob were both named in the East Caln tax list. Jacob Lockhart moved south to Augusta County, Virginia in 1738. John went there in 1744, the first of the Wards to do so. The closeness of the two families is further evidenced by the fact that James II's son James III married into the Lockhart family.

The Wards' and Lockharts' movements were more or less aligned with those of the flow of immigrants from Ireland. Waves of Scotch-Irish followed the Susquehanna River Valley from near the Maryland-Pennsylvania line northwest into the interior of Pennsylvania, then southeast along the Tuscarora mountain range into Maryland and Virginia.[5]

The population of immigrants moving west swelled during the peak years of migration. Sometime during the 1730s or early 1740s the Wards also moved farther west in Pennsylvania along the route of the Great Wagon Road. They settled onto property located a few miles north of the Road in Hopewell Township in Lancaster (now Cumberland) County. This was located on the Western Frontier, subject to Indian attack.

5. Ford, *Scotch-Irish*, 260–90.

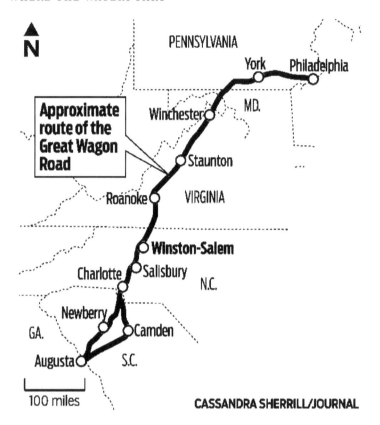

Figure 2. The Great Wagon Road from Philadelphia to the backcountry of Pennsylvania, Maryland, Virginia, the Carolinas, and Georgia.

A historical record from this time and place confirms a Ward's presence there. Their residence in Hopewell Township was just a few miles north of the town of Middle Spring. An entry from the session minutes of Middle Spring Presbyterian Church (1746) shows that a James Ward (James Ward II?) reported a neighbor's public drunken behavior to a church elder: "James Ward solemnly declared that at the vendue [public auction], he observed Samuel Laird, according to his judgment, staggering, whereupon he spoke to David Herron [ruling elder of the church] to persuade him to go home . . ."[6]

6. McElwain, *Genealogical Data*, 159, 171.

By today's standards, Ward's actions might be seen as meddling in another's affairs, not minding his own business, or gossiping, but by the communal standards of that time and place, by being an alert observer he would be helping maintain this frontier community's social order necessary for its survival. In this role, he would be acting authentically in the role of protector or guardian, for the community had to keep awake to the ever-present possibility of Indian attack. Of course, it is also true that these Scotch-Irish Presbyterians were known for strictness in enforcing high moral standards within their community. Disagreement about what behavior was allowed and what was not would often lead to congregational splitting.[7]

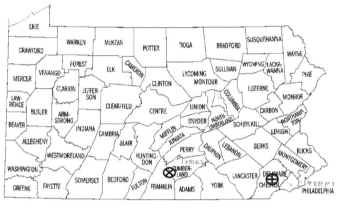

Figure 3. Pennsylvania, showing the location (x) of Middle Spring and Middle Spring Presbyterian Church, near James Ward's property (occupied through 1748) in Hopewell Township, Cumberland County, and the location (+) of the Wards' temporary settlement (in the early 1730s) soon after their arrival in America, in East Caln Township, Chester County.

7. "The splitting of the Presbyterians would be a nightmare for the lawyers who had to figure what church property belonged to whom. It wasn't just the Presbyterians who would split apart. This is the history of Christianity in America. . . . [In one congregation, it was reported that Virginia Presbyterian clergyman Dr. James] Waddell was brought up on charges for having hot coffee on the Sabbath, as well as other days. (The members were scandalized at his indulging in such luxury.) . . . How did our Presbyterian ancestors handle the schisms that caused their true church to split and split and split again? They became Baptists." Tracy, "Timber Ridge."

In addition to the church record just mentioned, historical evidence suggests this Ward family of English/Scottish heritage would have been closely identified with the Scotch-Irish Presbyterians, presumably church members like James II. Consider the following evidence.

The vast majority of the Scotch-Irish immigrants with whom the Wards traveled to America were members of the Presbyterian Church, a Christian denomination that had been founded by John Knox in Scotland during the Reformation in the sixteenth century, strongly influenced by Calvinism. Originally from Yorkshire in the English border region with Scotland, the Wards would have understood themselves to be dissenters from the Established Church (Episcopal or Church of England)—much like the Scottish Presbyterians and others who had also migrated to Ireland during the Ulster Plantation in the early seventeenth century.[8] We might speculate that before becoming fellow travelers with the Presbyterians, they may have identified themselves as Puritan Separatists. The Separatists, or Independents, were radical Puritans who hoped that the Established Church would reform itself of its "popish" rituals. Despairing of this possibility, they formed their own congregations. Some of them, perhaps also the Wards, left England for Ireland, much like the Pilgrims who left England for Amsterdam and then went to New England.

Second, John Ward married the daughter of a prominent Scottish Presbyterian family, the Campbells of Drumaboden, whose church membership is well documented in the eponymously titled book mentioned earlier.[9] The Wards (at least John Ward) are likely

8. "Many of the Episcopalian bishops in Ireland held religious views similar to those of the incoming Presbyterians. Like the Scots, these bishops were Puritans and believers in Calvinist theology. Since many of the parishes of the colony were without ministers, they allowed the Scottish ministers to join and [remain] within the pale of the Church of Ireland. . . . Thus, for some twenty years after the establishment of the Ulster Plantation, there was no religious persecution, and there were no separate Episcopal and Presbyterian Churches. The Irish Protestant Church was one and undivided." Chepesiuk, *Scotch-Irish*, 53–54.

9. Campbell, *Drumaboden* mentions that the later Campbells chronicled in that book were members of the Free Kirk of Scotland, a Reformed and

to have formally joined the Presbyterian Church sometime before John's marriage into this devout churchgoing family, which probably occurred before his emigration to America.

Third, we know that at least one of the Ward descendants, Captain James Ward IV (1763–1846), nephew of John and a Kentucky pioneer, was a Presbyterian church elder.

Despite the closeness we previously noted of the Scotch-Irish communities in Pennsylvania, life was becoming more difficult for all the settlers on the western frontier. Indian attacks were becoming more common. And as more arrivals from Ireland poured into the area, land prices increased. Many of the settlers continued moving to the south and west, attracted by cheaper land in Southwest Virginia offered by William Beverly, in partnership with the aforementioned John Lewis and James Patton, an offer intended mainly to attract the Scotch-Irish then living in Pennsylvania.

Beverly's Patent, also referred to as Beverly Manor, was granted by the governor to William Beverly in 1736 and consisted of 118,491 acres of land in Augusta County. It was divided up into many contiguous, undeveloped parcels, with special land deals offered to those settlers who could bring their friends and family along with them. However, after a few years, the attractions of the area wore thin as many of the early residents sold their land and moved even farther to the west or south. John Ward may have been an exception to this trend. But that is to get ahead of our story.

Evangelical offshoot (1843) from the Church of Scotland.

Figure 4. The John Lewis home on a farm known as Bellefonte in Beverly
Manor, Augusta County, near Staunton, Virginia. The stone (original)
portion was built about 1732.

In 1744, John went on ahead of the other members of the family,[10]
just as he had done before, to explore opportunities and perhaps
lay claim to land in Virginia made attractive by the low prices and
relative absence of conflict with Indians. Potential neighbors there
included some the Wards knew from the Old Country. The droves
of Scotch-Irish coming down to Virginia from Pennsylvania were
rapidly buying up land parcels in Beverly Manor (a huge area in
Augusta County containing the present-day town of Greenville,
southwest of Staunton, Virginia), or in the adjacent areas of the
Calfpasture River Valley or Borden's Grant.

In 1738, six years before John made his first appearance in
Augusta County, his wife Mary Ann's brother, Patrick Campbell,

10. By one account, John's wife Mary Ann Campbell died in Pennsylvania
the previous year (1743). If John was able to rely on other family members to
watch over his children, he would be free to serve as pathfinder into Virginia.

acquired a large parcel of 1,546 acres in Beverly Manor. That was the year land was first becoming available to new settlers. The size and date of the purchase indicate that Campbell probably intended to sell the land fairly soon, or at least sell portions of it, in return for a quick profit.

Ward family friends from Ireland and Pennsylvania, the Lockharts—James and his son Jacob—moved into Beverly Manor not long after Patrick Campbell did, Jacob purchasing land there in 1742 and Jacob's father James in 1748. Many other Campbells, Campbell in-laws, friends, and acquaintances from Ireland and Pennsylvania also moved to the area. Such coordinated movement into Pennsylvania and then Virginia was typical of Scotch-Irish migrations over the next century into what would later be called the backcountry of the United States.

John Ward's name shows up on a list of early settlers of the Calfpasture area in 1744, the year after it is thought his first wife, Mary Ann Campbell, died. But there is no record of his actually *purchasing* land anywhere in Augusta County at that time. Like many of the settlers coming into the area, he was probably squatting on someone else's land, presumably doing so with the owner's permission. Squatting seems to have been a common practice among the Scotch-Irish. But sometimes they did it without permission of the landowner.

From a land record we know that in 1750 John did buy a 231-acre parcel in Beverly Manor. This parcel happened to be a small piece of Patrick Campbell's original 1,546-acre purchase (although none of it was still owned by him at the time of John's acquisition).[11] From the record, we know that John bought the land from then-owner John Patterson. John likely invited his father, brothers, and extended family members to relocate from Pennsylvania to Southwest Virginia and live, at least temporarily, on the 231 acres. As mentioned before, conditions on the frontier in Pennsylvania were growing more difficult and would have provided a significant

11. Campbell's 1,546 acres were located in the southwestern corner of today's Greenville, Virginia, land containing the Broadhead Creek's confluence with the South River.

incentive for the Wards to move south by 1750. That was the year many of the settlers' dwellings were burned by order of the Quaker proprietors in an incident known as the "Burnt Cabins."[12]

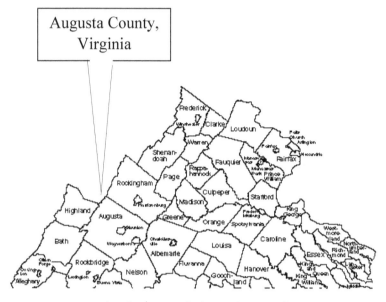

Figure 5. Virginia (northern portion), showing location of Augusta County

12. By May of 1750, the population of Cumberland County increased to the extent that the Indians complained to the proprietors in Philadelphia that treaties with them were being violated. The proprietors sided with the Indians and evicted the settlers, allowing their cabins to be burned. (This incident occurred in a place now identified by the name "Burnt Cabins," just twenty miles or so west of Middle Spring.) Havens, *Chambersburg*, 64.

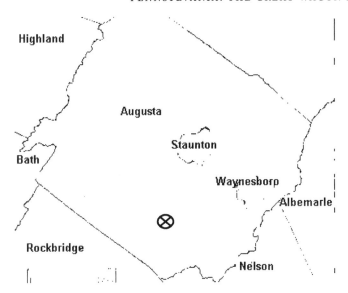

Figure 6. Augusta County, Virginia. Approximate location (x) of John Ward's 231 acres in Beverly Manor, south of Staunton, near present-day Greenville.

A land record notes that James II sold his property in Hopewell Township, Lancaster County (now Cumberland County), Pennsylvania on September 9, 1748 for £23.[13] We know from birth records as well as land records that Ward family members did indeed come down to Augusta County from Pennsylvania, although for the most part we don't have detailed information as to which ones went where and when they did so. Except for John Ward, they probably came down to Virginia sometime after the sale of the Hopewell Township property, but no later than 1755, when Indian attacks in Pennsylvania became especially severe.

James Ward "the Elder," James II, and James II's sons William and James III all made the trip to Virginia. James II's brother William (b. 1702) also moved to Virginia. That is established because William's sons David, John, William II, and James Lemill Ward were all born in Augusta County. (As would be a recurring theme

13. Egle, *Notes*. This property was near Middle Spring, Pennsylvania and Middle Spring Presbyterian Church, just north of Shippensburg, west of Harrisburg.

WHERE THE WATERS PART

of family occupations, David would become well known as an Indian fighter and cofounder of Russell County, Virginia, as well as justice of the peace and sheriff there, sometime in the 1770s.)

John's twenty-four-year-old nephew James III married Phoebe Lockhart in Augusta County in 1749, and their three sons, William, John, and James, were all born in Augusta County after 1750.[14] It seems likely they followed a pattern typical of the family, namely, that the heads of the households would each find property on which to settle, property sufficient to support themselves and their immediate (nuclear) family, located at a distance—but not too great a distance—from the others in the (extended) family. John would find such a place for himself in 1754, William in 1762.[15]

In May of that year, while retaining ownership of the 231-acre property, John purchased an additional 246-acre parcel in the neighboring Calfpasture Valley area. If he intended this new property to be designated as a place just for himself and his immediate family, he may have been neglecting his eighty-two-year-old father, increasingly frail and losing his eyesight, by then living alone on the 231 acres. John's new property was situated at the head of a tributary of the Little Calfpasture River known as Grassy Lick Run, near present-day Craigsville, Virginia. It was not far from the old property.

14. Captain James Ward III and his sons all enjoyed a measure of fame: the father for his role fighting and dying in the Battle of Point Pleasant (1774); the sons Colonel William Ward (b. 1752), for being a noted frontiersman, soldier, state militia officer, politician, merchant, and founder of Urbana, Ohio, and John "White Wolf" Ward (b. 1754), for being kidnapped by Indians at age three. John grew up as a Shawnee brave known as White Wolf and was tragically and unwittingly killed by his younger brother, Captain James Ward IV, in a battle at Paint Creek, Ohio, in 1793. (See Mattox,"Heaven," 2.) James Ward IV (b. 1763) was a noted wilderness explorer, Indian fighter, and legislator of Kentucky whose adventures featured prominently in widely circulated stories of the western frontier. He was a pallbearer at Daniel Boone's reinterment in 1845. He was also a Presbyterian elder.

15. On May 18, 1762, William purchased 279 acres in Borden's tract (thirty acres of which was "King's Land") in Augusta County. Chalkley, *Chronicles*, 384.

Evidence that the father was fending for himself in his last days is found in the sad petition he made to the Augusta County Parish in 1758, pleading for financial assistance. The appeal was made by "James Ward, 86 years old, almost blind and unable to provide for himself."[16] James Ward the Elder died later that same year. He is presumed buried in a churchyard somewhere in the Staunton, Virginia area.

In 1761, John sold the Calfpasture property and moved to nearby Jackson River, five miles to the west of present-day Warm Springs, Bath County, Virginia. At that time, John's nephew, James Ward III, had been living at Jackson River for three years, operating a mill there. This area would have been protected from Indian attack by nearby Fort Dinwiddie.

According to one source, in 1763 or shortly thereafter, John and his third wife, Mary McCormick, left Bath County and returned to Cumberland County, Pennsylvania, close to where he had lived nearly twenty years before. This area was now at peace following cessation of Indian attacks. That year, the Treaty of Paris brought the French and Indian War to a close. The Treaty allowed white settlers to legally own lands in that part of Pennsylvania and farther west, all the way to the Muskingum River in Ohio. When the Treaty went into effect, the hostile Indian incursions into the Path Valley, which had begun in 1755, ended. Some former settlers, including John Ward, took advantage of this opportunity to return to the Amberson Valley, located next door to the Path Valley. Many residents of Virginia, for one reason or another, grew restless and moved on, most of them heading west to such places as West Virginia, Kentucky, and Ohio. John, traveling north and east, moved against the general flow.

John Ward's grave is located on the edge of his land, in Stake Cemetery in the Amberson Valley, in present-day Franklin County, Pennsylvania. This county shares a border with present-day Cumberland County, including Hopewell Township, where James Ward II once owned property.

16. Chalkley, *Chronicles*, 446.

Ward family historian Paul McGowen believes that some family members continued to live on John's original Beverly Manor tract from 1750 until as late as 1775, the year that it was sold by John Ward Jr. [17] This was some eleven years after the senior John Ward returned to Pennsylvania, having fulfilled his pioneering and pathfinding duties on behalf of the Ward family.

John Ward was evidently born to be a pioneer, an explorer, and a trustworthy guide for his family, insuring their survival in a new and dangerous country. By accepting indentured servanthood at age twenty-four, John would have had to quickly demonstrate his value through his hard work, intelligence, and display of carpentry skills. His seriousness and ambition were attested to by his "marrying up" into the prominent Campbell clan. Besides his craftsmanship and work ethic, protecting his good name would have been essential for success. At the same time, being something of a free spirit, a creative and independent thinker, John revealed a restlessness observed in his many moves and relocations. John Ward, it would appear, found it hard to stay settled in one place for any length of time.

Only later in life, in his early sixties, did he discover that his heart's desire was to return to, and live peacefully in, the beautiful Amberson Valley of Franklin County, Pennsylvania, near today's Tuscarora State Forest in Fannett Township.[18] He purchased property there in 1766, next to the gently flowing waters of a creek named the South Branch of Laurel Run. I can imagine that John was able to enjoy the products of his life's labor that derived from

17. King, "John Ward," 56–60.

18. His return came after the earlier expulsion of white settlers in the "Burnt Cabins" incident of May 1750, subsequent to the peaceful purchase of land from the Indians in October 1758.

"The township was named after a place in County Donegal, Ireland, a promontory called 'Fannett Point.' This name was suggested by the shape of the township, a long, narrow point. Richard and John Coulter purchased a large body of land in the upper end of the township in 1756, and Francis Amberson made an improvement in Amberson's Valley in 1763. Then came Barnabas Clark, from whom 'Clark's Knob' receives its name, and *John Ward* and Cromwell McVitty. *These were the early and most prominent settlers of the valley*" (emphases added). Bates et al., *History*, 578.

the two stills he operated, his third wife, Mary McCormick, by his side (John perhaps operating those stills with the help of a son), until at last he died and was laid to rest in his little piece of heaven.

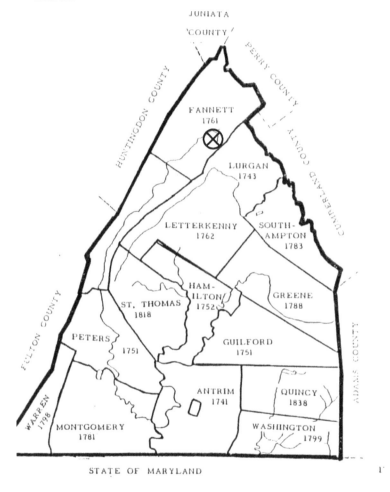

Figure 7. Franklin County, Pennsylvania. Approximate location (x) of John Ward's property (1766) on the South Branch of Laurel Run in the Amberson Valley, Fannett Township, in present-day Franklin County, Pennsylvania. Note the Irish place names.

JOHN WARD'S TIMELINE

[ ] indicates possible time/event

1704   John Ward is born in County Donegal, Ulster, Ireland.

[1726]   John marries Mary Ann Campbell (from the Campbell family of Drumaboden, Kilmacrenan, County Donegal).

[1727]   Son John Jr. is born.

1728   John arrives in Philadelphia as an indentured servant.

[1729–30]   Son Jacob is born, arrives in Philadelphia with his mother (perhaps with other family members?).

1738   1,546 acres is surveyed by brother-in-law Patrick Campbell near South River on the southwest edge of Beverly Manor.

1743   Daughter Elizabeth Jane is born in Cumberland County, Pennsylvania. (Mary Ann dies?)

1744   John Ward is listed as "an early settler" of the Calfpasture River Valley in Augusta County, Virginia. (John is the first of the Wards to arrive in Augusta County.)

1745   John is listed on Augusta Co. military service roll.

1750   John acquires 231 acres in Beverly Manor from John Patterson, part of 1,546 acres originally purchased by Patrick Campbell from William Beverly and his partners.

[1750–54]   John Ward marries Agnes _____.

1754   May 16. 246 acres is purchased in the Calfpasture River Valley.

1758   James Ward "the Elder" dies.

1761   John sells the land in the Calfpasture. Agnes is privately examined to insure fairness to her in this transaction.

1761   Fannett Township in Cumberland County, Pennsylvania is created.

[1761–63]   Agnes dies.

[1763–64]   John marries Mary McCormick.

1766   August 30. John Ward, or John Ward Jr., purchases 131 acres in Amberson Valley, Fannett Township and operates two stills on this land.

1775   March 20. John Jr. and his wife, Elizabeth, sell the 231 acres in Beverly Manor to John Sterling.

1784   Franklin County, Pennsylvania is established.

1786   John Ward, age eighty-two, appears on the list of Fannett Township's "taxables" for 1786.

[Aft. 1786]   John Ward dies and is buried next to his property, in Stake Cemetery, Fannett Township, Franklin County, Pennsylvania.

3

Virginia: Baptists Multiply, Families Divide

JOHN WARD AND MARY Ann Campbell's son, Jacob Ward (1730–1791), is said by some to have been born and lived his entire life in Culpeper County, Virginia. Another account says that he was born in Ireland or possibly even aboard a ship bound for America. Wherever he was born, by the time of his young adulthood and marriage in 1750, he had become a long-term resident of Culpeper County, a county that had been created the year before, in 1749, from what was originally part of Orange County, renamed Culpeper after its largest town. His early years were likely spent with his parents and other family members, first in Pennsylvania and then in Augusta County. It seems quite possible that he went to live in Culpeper County after his mother died, possibly in 1743.

What we do know for sure is that Jacob married Virginia "Anna" Hill of Culpeper about the time he went to live in an area of Culpeper County known as Little Fork. His purchase of land there was recorded by Lyman Chalkley in *Chronicles of the Scotch-Irish Settlement in Virginia, 1745–1800*: "May 17, 1750, William Hensley of St.Thomas Parish, Orange co, to Jacob Ward of Culpeper co, 200 acres in Little Fork on branches of the Rapidan River."[1]

Jacob operated a mill there in the fork created by the Robinson River's convergence with the Rapidan River (also known as the Rappadan River or the Rapid Ann River) in southwestern Culpeper County, near its border with Madison and Orange Counties.

Jacob seems to have been relatively prosperous. According to the 1787 census of Virginia, he owned six slaves. He was the first of the Wards, the first of three generations, to hold slaves.

Besides the location of his property, his marriage to Anna Hill, and information from his will, we don't know much about him except for a small but telling fact: Jacob, along with Culpeper County neighbors, signed a petition protesting a Virginia religious assessment bill, a bill sponsored by Patrick Henry.[2] The petition was dated November 2, 1785, appearing at an auspicious time in the church-state debate in postcolonial Virginia. Its signatories suggest divisions within the Ward and Hill families (if not others) in their views of religion and politics.

Figure 8. Virginia (northern portion), showing location of Culpeper County

1. Dorman, *Culpeper County Volume One*, 156–58.

2. "Protest."

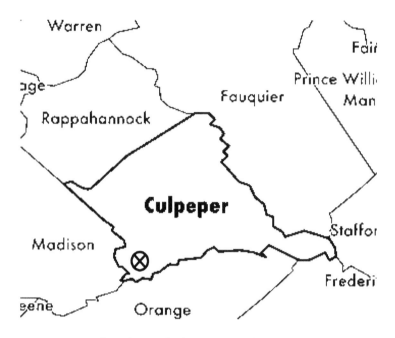

Figure 9. Little Fork area of Culpeper County (near the convergence of the
Robinson and Rapidan Rivers). Jacob Ward owned two hundred acres and
operated a mill here (x) after 1750.

Jacob's wife, Anna, was the daughter of a prominent family of Episcopalians, members of Christ Church Parish in Middlesex County,
Virginia. At some point, she and some of the other Hill family
members relocated from Middlesex to Culpeper County. The Hills
who went to Culpeper included Anna's older brother Russell and
Russell's son William. Jacob, Russell, and William were all cosign-
ers of the petition. The bill they were protesting was intended to
provide public support for "teachers of the Christian religion."

Public support for religion was widely thought to be essential
in the wake of the Church of England's disestablishment following
the Revolutionary War. The protesters' concern was *not* whether
Christianity should continue to be state supported—they were in
agreement with the bill's sponsor that it should be. Their concern
was rather that *if* state support was directed to *all* "teachers of the
Christian religion," *then*, in the protesters' view, the undesirable

"charismatic preachers" promoting evangelical Christianity would also receive state support. In their view, this was unacceptable. To support those preachers would serve to undermine true religion and would result in future generations of Virginians becoming, in the words of the petition, "Atheists, Deists, Idolaters, Infidels, or as other savage nations who have no laws relative to religion."

The Culpeper petition was careful to designate just which "teachers of the Christian religion" should be endorsed by the state and the manner of the endorsement. Candidates would be recommended by a panel drawn from each of six acceptable Christian denominations (Episcopal, Lutheran, Calvinist, Anabaptist, Methodist, Quaker). The candidates' names would then be submitted to the governor for approval.

While the petition did not mention by name any denomination for exclusion, Baptists were obviously excluded by *not* being named as one of the six. Why? Because they proselytized. It was no secret that Baptists would proselytize new members from other churches. The Baptists, however, saw this activity as evangelizing. They believed in the freedom of a person's conscience to hear and perhaps accept the gospel message (one freely offered to all who had ears to hear), preached by those whom God had called to preach, not by ministers licensed by the government.

Jacob and the other petition signers were therefore, by implication, opposed to state support of Baptists, but they were in favor of state support of other, acceptable forms of Christianity. But *any* public support of religion was anathema to supporters of church and state separation, like liberal politicians Madison and Jefferson and, of course, the Baptists. Liberals and Baptists were in agreement on this issue, but for different reasons. Liberals were against state promotion of religion; Baptists were for freedom of conscience, freedom to practice their religion, and freedom from persecution. Therefore, while the petition and the bill it protested ultimately failed, the arguments mounted against both of them ended up aiding the cause of church-state separation in the new United States of America.

Thus Jacob's signature on the petition in 1785 was clear indication of differences he had in the matters of religion and politics with his sons, John, William, and Jacob Jr., since no later than the 1780s they had all become Baptist church members, or at least by then they were all married into the Baptist church. (We know this since they were all married by Baptist ministers: John in 1779 in Surrey County—now Stokes County—North Carolina; William in 1782 in Culpeper County, Virginia; and Jacob Jr. in 1788 also in Culpeper County, Virginia). The fact that Jacob's signature on the petition appeared in the year 1785 is significant because at least the first two of these marriages occurred during a time of continuing persecution of the Baptists.[3]

Full freedom from religious discrimination in Virginia was only attained by passage of Thomas Jefferson's bill "Virginia Statute for Religious Freedom" in 1786, followed by Virginia's ratification of the U.S. Constitution with its First Amendment in 1788, not formally adopted in the United States until 1791.

The two older Ward brothers may have become Baptists during the six years before the Revolutionary War. The period in question, 1769–1775, was a time of great increase in the Baptists of Virginia. It coincided with a period of intense discrimination against them, especially notable in Culpeper County. Jacob's public stance against Baptists looks like it may have been the precipitating event before William's parting of ways with him about 1786, selling his land and moving down to Georgia with a bunch of like-minded neighbors. Younger brother Jacob Jr. also left Culpeper County about 1788, moving west to Woodford (now Scott) County, Kentucky. This area was part of Virginia until Kentucky became a state in 1792.

Oldest brother John had previously left Virginia for North Carolina some time prior to 1779. John Ward and Rachel Vernon were married there by a Reverend William Hill, probably a relative of Anna's. It was this William Hill (1700–1787), not the Ward in-law William Russell Hill, who had been for a period of time

3. It was not until June of 1784 that all marriages by dissenting ministers were declared valid by the House of Delegates.

disowned by his father (yet another William Hill) for becoming a Baptist, even a Baptist minister. His name was removed from the Christ Church baptismal register, either at his parents' or his own request.[4]

The two couples, William Ward and Sarah Vernon (Rachel's cousin), and Jacob Ward Jr. and Sally Quinn, were married by a local Baptist minister, George Eve. Eve, reputedly one of Culpeper's most "charismatic" preachers, was at that time a part-time pastor of Rapidan Baptist Church in Wolftown, one of the first Separate Baptist churches in Virginia. He divided his time between pastoring at Rapidan and at another Culpeper County church, F. T. Baptist Church at Sperryville. The two couples may have been associated with one of those churches, if not members.

William's marriage occurred in December 1782, almost exactly one year to the day after he was discharged from his war service and three years before Jacob signed the petition in 1785. William and Sarah moved south to Georgia about a year after the signing. Jacob Jr. and Sally moved west to Kentucky about two years after that, about 1788, to Lebanon (now Georgetown), Kentucky (home of Elijah Craig's Great Crossing Church.)[5] These events do not seem to have been coincidental.

It is clear that Anna's parents, William Russell Hill and Ann Needles Hill were staunch members of the Church of England (Anglicans) prior to its disestablishment, having both been baptized and married in Christ Church Parish, Middlesex County. William Russell Hill was descended from generations of Hills who were parishioners there. (It is not known where or by whom Anna and Jacob were married, but circumstances suggest their marriage took place in Christ Church Parish or in another Anglican parish in Culpeper County.) In 1785, then, Jacob's sympathies would seem to have been aligned with Episcopalians (former Church of

4. Hill, "Early Hills."

5. Elijah Craig (1743–1808) was ordained in 1771 in Virginia at Blue Run (Separatist) Baptist Church in Orange County. He migrated to Kentucky in 1782, the year after his brother Louis Craig led as many as six hundred people to Kentucky from Spotsylvania County, Virginia. They were known as "The Travelling Church."

England members) and against the Baptists, who claimed the allegiance of his sons, John, William, and Jacob Jr., a certain James Ward (who, I believe, may be Jacob Sr.'s nephew),[6] and the Reverend William Hill.

Jacob and Anna also had a strong familial bond with Anna's brother, Russell Hill, another indication of their affinity with the Hill family. A Culpeper County record of May 15, 1760 describes a notable gift that Russell gave to the couple early in their marriage: "Russell Hill of Brumfield Parish, Culpeper co to Jacob Ward and Ann his wife of same, for natural and brotherly affection he doth bear unto his brother-in-law Jacob Ward and his sister Anne Ward, wife of Jacob Ward, [and] one Negro girl, Nan . . ."[7]

Why did so many of this generation of Wards who came of age during or shortly after the Revolutionary War become Baptists? Of course we will never know what was in their heads or hearts at the time. Many factors were at play. The American Revolution was all about freedom: economic freedom, religious freedom, and freedom from oppression by the existing social order. The Baptists spoke to these freedoms, most powerfully to those who felt discriminated against by the existing order. The Separate Baptists, the church with which these Wards were associated, tended to be against slavery and more accepting of African-Americans as church members than other churches such as the Regular Baptists. The Separates parted ways with the Regulars in response to the Great Awakening revivals.[8] The Revolution was also about living authentically in the sense that each individual was now free to live according to the truth and in pursuit of happiness, as they understood these things, not as prescribed by a sovereign.

Baptists appealed directly to the conscience of the adult believer, albeit a conscience informed by the truth they understood from the Bible and under conviction by the Holy Spirit. The appeal of Baptists was in this way an appeal to fidelity to oneself, an appeal

6. Perhaps this was James Ward IV, son of Captain James Ward III.

7. Transaction witnessed by Richard Vawter. Clearly this is a reference to slave ownership. Dorman, *Culpeper County Volume Two*, 343-44.

8. Bebbington, *Baptists*, 76.

to true self-fulfillment, within the guardrails of a Baptist tradition. This contrasted with other Christian traditions, especially those practicing infant baptism, such as the Presbyterian and the Episcopal traditions. Baptism in those traditions signified joining the church family according to the will of the child's family and church community, an act to be later confirmed by the child after she reached the age of consent.

The (First) Great Awakening's influence spread from New England to the South in the decades prior to the Revolutionary War. In 1751, Shubal Stearns, pastor of a Separate (Congregational) church in Tolland, Connecticut, was baptized, became a Baptist, and traveled south to Virginia to preach with his brother-in-law, Daniel Marshall. Originally a Presbyterian, Marshall had been influenced by the revival preaching of George Whitefield.[9] Marshall also became a Baptist. In 1755, Stearns and Marshall established a Separate Baptist church in Sandy Creek, North Carolina, which became the mother church of a new association of Separate Baptists in the South. The Separates, whose Calvinism was more nuanced than that of the Regular Baptists,[10] multiplied rapidly, bringing the evangelical and emotional fervor of the Great Awakening into Virginia and Culpeper County. Their increase was especially great during the period 1769–1775, just prior to the Revolutionary War.

Many of the new Baptist converts had been members of the Church of England, including the Reverend William Hill and, presumably, the younger generation of Wards, whose parents were most likely members of the established church. If so, it is reasonable to think they would have been baptized as adults before they were married in Baptist ceremonies.

So if these assumptions are correct, it might be said that it was through a parting of the waters of an adult "believer's baptism" that

9. One of the initiators of the Great Awakening (with John Wesley).

10. They were influenced by Jonathan Edwards and his argument concerning the "natural will" vs. the "moral will" in his *magnum opus, Freedom of the Will*. The natural will could be appealed to by the evangelist even if the moral will was corrupted by sin.

a generation of Wards separated themselves from their religious heritage and found a pathway to a new life with their fellow believers, to a "heaven on Earth." For them, the baptismal waters would have opened the way in their search for freedom and authenticity.

The rapid growth of the Baptist churches and their converts was bound to provoke a strong backlash against them. This was especially true of the Separate Baptists, who, being the most evangelical of the anti-establishment churches, were the main targets of persecution.[11] Persecution came from those religious and political conservatives who saw their privileged place in society steadily eroding, namely, and in particular, the Anglicans.

The following account of physical violence directed against Baptists provides a vivid description of this persecution:

> In Virginia, religious persecution, directed at Baptists and, to a lesser degree, at Presbyterians, continued after the Declaration of Independence. The perpetrators were members of the Church of England, sometimes acting as vigilantes but often operating in tandem with local authorities. Physical violence was usually reserved for Baptists, against whom there was social as well as theological animosity. A notorious instance of abuse in 1771 of a well-known Baptist preacher, "Swearin Jack" Waller, was described by [one of]the victim[s]: "The Parson of the Parish [accompanied by the local sheriff] would keep running the end of his horsewhip in [Waller's] mouth, laying his whip across the hymn book, etc. When done singing [Waller] proceeded to prayer. In it he was violently jerked off the stage; they caught him by the back part of his neck, beat his head against the ground, sometimes up and sometimes down, they carried him through the gate . . . where a gentleman [the sheriff] gave him . . . twenty lashes with his horsewhip.
>
> The persecution made a strong, negative impression on many patriot leaders, whose loyalty to principles of civil liberty exceeded their loyalty to the Church of England in which they were raised. James Madison was not the only patriot to despair, as he did in 1774, that

11. Bailess, "Samuel Harris," 2.

the "diabolical Hell conceived principle of persecution rages" in his native colony. Accordingly, civil libertarians like James Madison and Thomas Jefferson joined Baptists and Presbyterians to defeat the campaign for state financial involvement in religion in Virginia. [12]

As far as is known, Jacob's sons did not themselves experience such extreme forms of persecution. Despite differences Jacob may have had with his sons, in the end, he demonstrated fairness toward them by leaving a will in which William, then a married man with four young children and recently relocated to Georgia, was the chief beneficiary, even though William was not the oldest of Jacob's children. (John was the oldest but third in order of the amount of monetary inheritance, following that of William and Jacob Jr. The youngest son, Mitchell, was fourth.) Jacob's will was proved and recorded by the Culpeper Court on June 20, 1791:

> In the name of God amen I Jacob Ward of Culpeper County do make this my last will and Testament. I inpass [sic] it and recommenced [sic] [my?] soul to almighty God hoping for pardons and forgiving all my sins through the trials and meditations of our Blessed Savior Jesus Christ. Item I leave to my beloved wife Anne Ward estate both real personal during her natural life as widowhood and after her death or marriage to be divided in the following manner. Item I give to my son John Ward fifteen pounds fifteen shillings in sundry articles. Item I give to my son William Ward twenty eight pounds thirteen shillings in six pence in sundry articles. Item I give to my son Jacob Ward eighteen pounds eighteen shillings and six pence in sundry articles. Item I give to my son Mitchell Ward ten pounds in sundry articles. Item I give to my Daughter Franky Vawter four pounds sixteen shillings and six pence in sundry articles. Item I give to my Daughter Judah Ward eleven pounds seventeen shillings and four pence in sundry articles. Item I give to my Daughter Anne Ward one Bed and Saddle at seven pounds. Item I give to my Daughter Sarah Yager during her life on a Childs part of my Estate and after her death

12. "Religion."

to go to her Daughter Anne Rodifer. Item my will and desire is that my son Mitchell Ward shall have one Bed at seven pence price. Item my will and desire is that the rest of my children shall be in and Equal (to) my Son William Ward and after all my children is made Equal with William Ward thru then the whole of my Estate both real and personal shall be Equally divided between all my children or their legal representatives————-

I nominate and appoint William Booten and Hadley Heucht executors of this my last will and testament hereby making all other wills heretofore by me made declaring this only to be my last will and testament on ——— where I hereto set my hand and affixed my seal this thirty fourth day of March one thousand seven hundred and ninety one.

Signed Sealed & Published as my last Will & Testament.

Signed Jacob Ward

witnesses: Mildred Heucht   Mary Heucht[13]

In retrospect, Jacob's primary concern appeared to be maintaining the good order and traditions of the Culpeper community, showing himself to be a responsible citizen supporting institutional Christianity, the basis of civil society as it was then in Virginia. There was no evidence he participated in the abuse of Baptists or other dissenters. Despite his deliberate snub of the Baptists by supporting the Culpeper petition, he was evidently concerned to be fair to all his children, whatever their decision in regard to their church, judged by the will's provision that "the rest of my children shall be . . . equal (to) my Son William Ward."

Jacob was evidently less interested than his father or his sons in searching for adventure and freedom. He lived his whole life as a citizen of Culpeper County. There is no record of his living anywhere else. It appears he preferred to continue living in the Anglican tradition rather than follow a new tradition like that of the emotional, enthusiastic, free-spirited Separate Baptists that had captured the allegiance of the next generation of Wards.

13. W. Ward, "Last Will."

It seems likely that oldest son John's decisions to enter the military, marry within the Baptist Church, and relocate some distance away from Culpeper into a like-minded community almost certainly influenced his younger brothers William and Jacob Jr. to take these same actions,[14] relocating to North Carolina, Georgia, and Kentucky, respectively. The last brother, Mitchell, two years younger than Jacob Jr., apparently followed him to Kentucky. They were both listed on the 1790 tax list for Woodford (later Scott) County Kentucky, two years after Jacob Jr. married Sally Quinn in Culpeper County. There is no record of Mitchell marrying in Virginia prior to his relocating to Kentucky.[15]

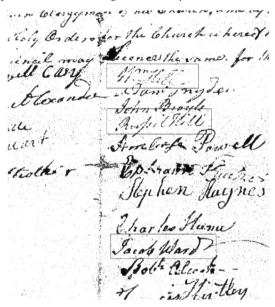

Figure 10. Culpeper Petition to the Virginia General Assembly (November 2, 1785), detail showing, respectively, the signatures of William Hill (son of Russell Hill), Russell Hill (Jacob's brother in law) and Jacob Ward, in the top, middle, and bottom boxes, respectively.

14. With one exception, Jacob Jr. (b. 1766). He was too young to serve in the Revolutionary War.

15. Both Jacob Jr. and Mitchell may have followed Baptist leader Rev. Elijah Craig (1743–1808) from Culpeper to Woodford County. In 1786 Craig established the Great Crossing Church near the newly incorporated town of Lebanon, whose name was changed to Georgetown in 1790.

JACOB WARD'S TIMELINE

[ ] indicates possible time/event

1730   Jacob Ward is born [in Ireland? onboard ship to America? in Culpeper?].

1750   Jacob marries Virginia "Anna" Hill, daughter of William Russell Hill, member of St. Mark's Parish, Middlesex County, Virginia. Jacob purchases property in Culpeper County.

1750   Jacob operates mill on branches of the Rapidan River, at Little Fork by the mouth of the Robinson River.

1755   Son John Ward is born.

1757   Son William Ward is born.

1761   Son Jacob Ward Jr. is born.

1763   Son Mitchell Ward is born.

1775–83   Jacob serves as private in the Virginia Continental Troops.

1785   Jacob signs the Culpeper petition against the Virginia religious assessment bill sponsored by Patrick Henry.

1787   Census of Virginia shows that Jacob Ward owns six slaves.

1791   Jacob Ward dies. Anna Hill Ward dies.

4

Georgia: Led by "the Spirit of Migration"

JACOB WARD'S SECOND-OLDEST SON, William, was born in Culpeper County in 1757, following the birth of his older brother John in 1755. Changes in the brothers' religious affiliations and resulting tensions within the family suggested a possible motive for them to leave Virginia for greener pastures elsewhere. Is it possible to discover, or at least speculate, about what may have influenced them to relocate to the places they went? We will concentrate on William's story (since he is in the direct line of Wards we are following in this book), but we also know more about him from a detailed record he provided of his service in the Revolutionary War. Besides that, there are a number of similarities between the brothers' stories.

William Ward was a Continental Army soldier during two periods, March 9, 1776—March 10, 1778 and July 1, 1780—December 31, 1781, in the first period with rank of private and in the second with rank of sergeant. Most notably, he was with George Washington at Valley Forge during the infamous winter he spent there.

The following account summarizes William's movements during the War, based on details he provided in his pension application submitted on September 19, 1832:

> William enlisted under Lieutenant Busby, transferred to Captain Francis Taylor's Company of the 2nd Virginia Regiment at Williamsburg under Colonel William Spotswood. He spent the first winter [of 1776–1777] in Morristown, New Jersey. William was a participant at the Battle of Brandywine on September 11, 1777 and at the Battle of Germantown on October 4, 1777. He spent the winter of 1777–1778 at Valley Forge. He was discharged on March 13, 1778. He again enlisted on July 1, 1780 as a substitute for John Payne in the militia and was appointed sergeant under Captain Oldham. He went from Culpepper County to Chesterfield Courthouse, Virginia, where Colonel Campbell took command. His unit was placed under the command of General Nathaniel Green. William fought at the Battle of Guilford Courthouse and again participated at the Battle of Camden, South Carolina against Lord Rawdon on April 25, 1781. William then went to Ninety-Six, South Carolina and took part in the Siege of Camden. William's unit then marched to Eutaw Springs where he participated in the Battle of Eutaw Springs that was fought there. He was discharged on December 31, 1781.[1]

According to one reporter's estimate,[2] William walked more than two thousand miles during his military service in the War. Soon after his second military discharge, he married Sarah Vernon in Culpeper, Virginia on December 19, 1782.[3]

1. W. Ward, "Probate Records."

2. Harrison, "Remembering."

3. Sarah's grandfather Thomas Vernon Sr. (1686–1756) was "'disowned' by the Quaker meeting in Chester County, Pennsylvania in 1709/10 for "his vain and evil conversation as that of drinking to excess, loose company keeping, cursing, swearing, and lying." He went to Cub Creek, Virginia in 1737 and became a Presbyterian. His father had originally come to Pennsylvania with William Penn and appears to have disowned the son. Sarah was born in 1764 in Bromfield Parish, Culpeper, Culpeper County, Virginia, daughter of Richard Vernon (1711–1795), son of Thomas Vernon Sr. and Sarah Tinsley

William and Sarah initially lived on Virginia land given them by Sarah's father, Richard Vernon, on November 14, 1783, land next to a creek known as Smith's Run (now White Oak Run), which flows into the Robinson River, a tributary of the Rapidan River, in Southwest Culpeper County. William, like his father, operated a mill. His was located a few miles north of Jacob's at Little Fork.

As compensation for his War service, William received a "bounty land grant" from Virginia on January 16, 1786 for one hundred acres. It is likely that he sold this grant rather than acquiring more property in Virginia, because just a few months later, on August 4, 1786, William and Sarah sold their land on Smith's Run to Simeon Buford and left Virginia, relocating to Coldwater Creek in Elbert County (formerly Wilkes County), Georgia. Coldwater Creek is a tributary of the Savannah River, and this is where William found an ideal place to situate another mill. William's and Sarah's six children were born in Virginia and in Georgia. Their son Abner Ward, whose story we follow, was born in Georgia in 1787.

What caused these Wards to move to Georgia, the last stop on the Great Wagon Road, leaving Virginia at this particular time? A clue comes from a land record showing their Virginia neighbor George Alexander moving from Culpeper to (what was then) Wilkes County, Georgia sometime between 1783 and 1786, or shortly before William relocated there. (George Alexander would later become a Ward in-law. He was the grandfather of Robert Burke Alexander, who married Sarah Livonia Ward, one of Abner's daughters.) The Alexanders, as it happened, were but one of numerous Ward neighbors from the same part of Virginia relocating to Wilkes/Elbert County.

Besides the Alexanders, their new neighbors in Georgia included many others they already knew from Culpeper County.[4] As we have noted, although separation of church and state became

(1722–1825). Though born into the Episcopal Church, she was of Quaker and Presbyterian heritage.

James, "Thomas Vernon."

4. "CulpeperAlexanders"

law in Virginia in 1786, it did not become law in the United States until the First Amendment was approved in 1791. It is reasonable to think these neighbors, many of them Baptists, may have thought it advantageous to leave Culpeper County, where they were still being persecuted, and find their way into the frontier land of Georgia, to a place where they could live in freedom and peace, away from the Episcopalians and the Presbyterians, to a place of their own.

Another clue to William's choice of Georgia destination comes from a Baptist minister's church record. It suggests the relocation was a coordinated event, that is, a group migration from Culpeper to Elbert County, Georgia. This church record refers to a migration that happened at about the same time the Wards left Virginia. George Eve, the Baptist minister who married William and Sarah Vernon in 1782 and Jacob Jr. and Sally Quinn in 1788, wrote the following memorial in the front of one of the church minute books of the Rapidan Baptist Church (1796): "The spirit of migration took place at the Ragged Mountains, many of our members emigrated to Georgia and Kentucky. Some of our members excommunicated in the beginning of the year 1788 . . ."

It seems likely, from the Wards' association with Eve, that they were also associated in some way with the congregation at Rapidan or with one of the other Baptist churches that sprang up in the Culpeper area in the pre-War years. Eve, for instance, ministered at both Rapidan and F. T. in 1782, the year he officiated at William's and Sarah's marriage.[5]

Eve's connection with these churches tells us much about the attitudes of its members. He was an important figure in the rise of the Separate Baptists in the backcountry of Virginia after its encounter with the (First) Great Awakening. As mentioned previously, the Separate Baptists were more enthusiastic and evangelical compared with the more numerous Regular Baptists. The Regulars were more strictly Calvinist in their views, more somber

---

5. Baptist congregations in the Culpeper area beginning about this time were Blue Run Church, planted in 1769; Rapidan, planted in 1773; Mount Pony, planted in 1774; and F. T., planted in 1778.

in outlook, less accepting of the Separates' enthusiasm, and disapproving of their theological view that sinful man possessed a natural will that was free to respond to God's leading.

Eve's expression "the spirit of migration," written in the Rapidan Baptist Church minute book, may have suggested that something more was involved for these Baptists' removal from Virginia to points south or east than running away from persecution or seeking inexpensive land on the frontier. It meant, quite possibly, that they believed they had heard a call from God indicating that, like Israel, they should follow God's leading to a new land of freedom and promise. And that new land, for William and Sarah and for many of their Virginia neighbors, was Georgia. According to Eve's record, they heard this call before their exodus in 1788, the same year that Georgia became a state.

William's father Jacob died in 1791, five years after William's departure from Virginia. His father's death closed a chapter in his life. However, he would have had other family members from whom he could draw inspiration for his life, in particular, his grandfather and his older brother.

When William was a boy, he would have heard tales of his grandfather John's pioneering exploits blazing a trail for the family to follow from Ireland to Pennsylvania and then down to Virginia. No doubt, these tales were full of adventure, full of fear from Indian attacks, and full of joy from successes. William, now a veteran of the Revolutionary War like his older brother John, must have been brimming with confidence that he could both survive and flourish in a new environment. In this confidence he was probably very different from his apparently more conservative father Jacob.

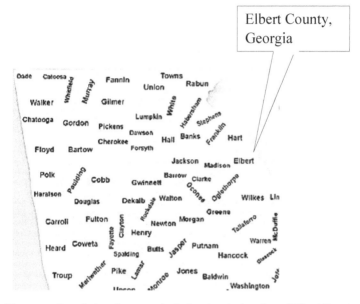

Figure 11. Georgia (northern portion), showing the location of Elbert County.

Figure 12. Elbert County, Georgia, 1823, showing the approximate location
of William Ward's land and gravesite by Coldwater Creek, above the
Savannah River.

Following their move to Georgia, William and Sarah became associated with Van's Creek Baptist Church in Elbert County. Furthermore, it is known that they were slave owners. A record from the church (1801) notes that "a black woman named Bridget belonging to William Ward" was received into membership "by experience" on December 11. The Separate Baptists mentioned previously, with whom Van's Creek identified,[6] were generally against slavery and welcomed new black members. However, that did not mean that members were required to free their slaves. But the members must have surely been aware that their recent struggle for freedom from England and commitment to their own religious beliefs had negative implications for the practice of slavery.

William was the second of three generations of Ward slave holders of record. William's son Abner was apparently the last. Abner, we know, had some association with Van's Creek in that he would marry a young woman, Frances Julia Kidd, whose family were long-time dedicated members of Van's Creek Baptist Church: the Webb Kidds.

William applied for a soldier's pension in 1832, many years after his move to Georgia. The pension application, as we saw, provided a detailed account of William's actions and movements during the War. It shows that he still had a good memory of details dating back more than fifty years. But within twenty years of his application, in 1850, William would be declared incompetent by a Georgia lunacy commission. In that year he attained the ripe old age of ninety-two, a rare accomplishment in those days. His declared "lunacy" was most likely what we would today call an age-related dementia. Daughter Sarah V. "Sally" Haley subsequently assumed legal responsibility for her father and was named as his guardian by order of the Inferior Court.

William's gravesite is today marked by a Daughters of the American Revolution (DAR) plaque located near William's and Sarah's burial plots. The plots lie beneath stone boxes located on a small hill on the edge of their former property on Coldwater Creek, near its confluence with the Savannah River. Names and dates are still barely visible on the worn surfaces of the stones.

6. Scott, *History*, 155.

Figure 13. DAR grave marker of William Ward (1757–1850).

Figure 14. Graves of William and Sarah Ward.

Coldwater Creek's shoreline has now greatly expanded since the 1985 construction of the Richard B. Russell Dam. The Wards' former property containing the gravesite now lies in a beautiful wooded area known as Patriot's Point.

When considered within the context of Ward family history and that of the United States, William Ward's will[7] provides a rich source of information about family relationships as well as possible motives for various decisions taken by William and other family members. The will named executors William R. Haley (Sally's husband) and William Buffington (husband of Sally's daughter Millie). It was filed in June of 1844 in Elbert County, Georgia when William was nearly eighty-seven years of age, probably already in failing health due to the onset of dementia. It is clear from the will that, though she was not named executor, Sally still played a critical role as guardian in helping William attend to his affairs during his last days.

William, per custom of the testator, proclaimed that in making his will, he was "of sound mind & disposing memory." This became an important issue in that within a relatively short period of time (six years), by early 1850, the justices of the Inferior Court, "sitting as a Court of Ordinary" in Elbert County, had pronounced William "an insane person" and received bond payment in the amount of $7,000 as surety for Sally V. Haley's faithful execution as William's guardian. (Treatment of mentally ill persons in Georgia had progressed to the extent that in 1837 a "lunacy commission" was created to properly classify mentally ill persons as "lunatics" or "insane persons." This was not to segregate them from society but to ensure their legal protection.)

At the time of his death in 1850, William left the bulk of his property to his two daughters, Sally V. Haley and Nancy Butler, property consisting primarily of William's land, buildings on the north and south side of Coldwater Creek, along with major kitchen and bedroom furniture as well as four slaves and a horse. The meager collection of remaining items he directed to be distributed "equally amongst all my children then living and the

7. W. Ward, "Last Will," 6–7.

children of those that now are or may then be dead after paying all my just debts, funeral expenses and other necessary expenses of my estate . . ."

By the time the will was written in 1844, three of William's sons (Abner, Richard, and William H.) were already dead, leaving only son Austin and daughters Judith, Nancy, and Sally. William's grandchildren whose fathers were dead by that time (there were by my count at least twelve) could well have outnumbered his own children still living. In particular, among these grandchildren, at least three were of minor age when their father died: Lawrence L., Mildred E., and John C., these three being children of Abner and his wife, Frances Julia "Franky" Kidd. (Abner died at age fifty in 1837.) Specifically, these three children were eight years of age or younger when their father died.

It seems surprising then that they were not named but only indirectly mentioned along with his surviving children in the will. That may have been due to the complications that by 1848 both of the minor grandchildren's parents were dead, and three years before his death Abner had inexplicably abandoned his family and taken up residence with a French woman with whom he proceeded to have three more children, and he did this without benefit of a divorce from Franky or a remarriage. This Ward family scandal—complicated by Abner's dying intestate and William's being declared an "insane person"—seems a development ripe for legal dispute over Abner's estate, a process that in fact went on for years after his death in December 1837.

Wife Franky, publicly humiliated and with no provision of support from her late husband's will (because it didn't exist), went to court seeking support from his estate, including support for her three youngest children, which she arranged to be cared for (out of the public eye?) in Alabama by a court-appointed guardian, William Johnston. It seems surprising she didn't join her children there, except for the fact she still had older children still in Georgia as well as other family members living there.

Interestingly, and perhaps showing that he was likely anticipating future disputes after his death, William stated in the will that his motive for leaving the largest portion of the estate to daughter Sally was "to make her share equal to what I have heretofore given the others & to compensate her for having stayed with and taken care of me & attended to my business & household affairs."[8] He surely wanted to be fair, first of all, to his many children, so that provision for the grandchildren was not at the top of his mind. That would certainly be unusual, as not many people lived to his advanced age in those days, and he lived longer than many of his children. Grandchildren should—in the usual course of things—be provided for by their own parents, even if in this case (that of the minor grandchildren mentioned above) it took an order from the court to make it happen.

WILLIAM WARD'S TIMELINE

1757	August 12. William Ward is born in Culpeper County, Virginia to Jacob Ward and Anna Hill Ward.
1776	March 9. William enlists as a private in the Continental Army in Culpeper.
1778	March 10. William is discharged from the Army.
1780	May 15. William purchases fifty-four acres from John James. Land is located on the Hazel River in Culpeper County.
1780	July 1. William re-enlists as a substitute.
1781	December 31. William is discharged with rank of sergeant.
1782	December 19. William marries Sarah Vernon in Culpeper, Virginia. Baptist minister George Eve officiates.

8. W. Ward, "Last Will," 6–7.

1783	November 14. William and Sarah receive 116.5 acres on Smith's Run as a gift from Sarah's father, Richard Vernon.
1786	August 4. William and Sarah sell the 116.5 acres to Simeon Buford.
1786	William and family move to Elbert County, Georgia.
1832	September 19. William applies for war pension, signed with his signature (not with an "X").
1837	Son Abner Ward dies intestate.
1844	June 1. William's will is filed in Elbert County, Georgia, this time signed with his "X" and witnessed.
1849	Court authorizes payment (of $35) to the Commission of Lunacy for trying the case of William's "alleged insanity."
1850	January 22. Sarah V. "Sally" Haley (William's daughter) is appointed William's guardian. William is identified as "an insane person."
1850	March 12. William dies in Elberton, Georgia, age ninety-two.
1850	December 3. County Court certifies list of items to be sold from William's estate.
1854	August 7. Court permits will executors (William Buffington and William R. Haley) to sell William's land except for what was explicitly granted (to daughters Sarah V. Haley and Nancy J. Butler).
1855	Payment ($6) to Asa Chandler, preacher at William's funeral.
1857	December 20. Payment ($4) to William R. Haley for "helping to hall [sic] the rock to wall William Ward's grave."[9]

9. W. Ward, "Probate Records," 6–7.

ABNER VERNON WARD

As touched upon previously, William's son Abner, apparently an otherwise upstanding and prosperous member of the Elbert County community, abandoned his family about 1834, lived with a French woman named Patricia Arquette, with whom he had three more children (Richard Ward, Robert Ward, and James J. Ward), and died intestate in late 1837. There is no record of a divorce ever having been granted to Abner Ward and Franky Kidd for the dissolution of their marriage, nor any indication of the circumstances of the abandonment. Abner appeared to have been materially successful judging from the sizable inventory of his property disposed of by the probate court. Nevertheless, his life became an unfortunate example of one going "off the rails." He clearly had not been a responsible person in his actions toward his wife and children, nor had he been able to avoid the public scandal that followed. Fortunately, Franky, with the cooperation of the estate's executor, was able to ensure provision for her and her family despite the absence of a will. In particular, they were able to ensure that the three youngest children would receive their education, in Shelby County, Alabama, located just south of Birmingham.[10] Besides the court-named guardian, Thomas Johnston, Franky had Kidd family relatives in Alabama who could help her watch over these children.

The oldest of the three was Lawrence L. Ward, whose story we follow in the next chapter.

ABNER V. WARD'S TIMELINE

[ ] indicates possible time/event

1787   October 27. Abner Vernon Ward is born in Culpeper County, Virginia.

---

10. Franky was the daughter of Webb Kidd, a long-time member of Van's Creek Baptist Church. She would likely have made sure that her children faithfully attend church and Sunday school and receive their basic education.

1807   December 24. Abner marries Frances Julia Kidd in Elbert County, Georgia. They have thirteen children (including one, Frances, who died at birth).

[1834?]   Abner leaves the family, goes to live with Patricia Arquette; three more children are born.

1837   December. Abner V. Ward dies intestate in Elbert County, Georgia. The three youngest of his children with Frances (Lawrence L. Ward, Mildred L. Ward, and John C. Ward) are listed as "minor children of Abner Vernon Ward" in Elbert County, Georgia. The oldest of the three is Lawrence Lafayette ("L. L."), age eight.

1848   September 9. Frances Julia Kidd Ward dies in Elbert County, Georgia.

5

North Texas 1:
Pioneer, Defender, Judge

LAWRENCE LAFAYETTE "L. L." Ward was old enough at twenty, by the time his ninety-two-year-old Revolutionary War veteran grandfather William died on March 12, 1850, that the grandfather most assuredly would have exerted a strong influence on the young man as he grew up. That was especially true because L. L.'s father, Abner, had been mostly *in absentia*, living apart from the family for some years before his early death in 1837.

The boy would, without question, have heard thrilling first-person accounts of William's adventures as a soldier in battles all up and down the American colonies, including the tale of a bitterly cold winter spent at Valley Forge with George Washington, as well as the story of a post-War journey with a young family adventuring south from Virginia to begin a new life in Georgia.

William's stories—with their vivid accounts of war, courage, self-reliance, and dedication to the revolutionary cause of freedom, and of self-determination in matters of politics and religion—were narratives of events occurring when the grandfather was himself a young man in his twenties (the same age as L. L. was in 1850, more than seventy years later).

Having such a grandfather to inspire him would not, of course, make up for a father missing in action during most of the prior fifteen years and the disruption of his early life in Georgia. Throughout his young adult life spent in Alabama, L. L. must have had recurring feelings of insecurity from the loss of the life he had known in Elbert County, difficult though it had been.

The father, Abner Ward (age forty-two when this son was born), had been absent from L. L.'s life on two counts: In 1834, when the son was five, Abner left his family to live with another woman, even starting a second family with her; three years later, when L. L. was eight, the father died intestate, that is, without leaving a will, allowing his property to be divided by decision of the Inferior Court of Elbert County through the legal process known as probate. The proceeds of the estate were distributed over several years to those who could present justifiable claims to the court; numerous creditors and older siblings waited their turn to be paid.

After their father's death, L. L. and his younger sister and brother, Millie and John, were sent out of the state to live with guardian Thomas Johnston in Shelby County, Alabama. Their mother was at that time still living in Georgia. (She had blood relatives living in that part of Alabama, a fact that probably influenced her decision to send the young children there.) Johnston also happened to be administrator of Abner's estate. While exercising his responsibilities as guardian, he made sure that he was properly reimbursed for every itemized expense he submitted to the court on behalf of the Ward children. These expenses included the cost of their clothes and their schooling. Being minors, the children apparently received no inheritance directly from Abner's estate. But they seemed to be well taken care of, at least materially and educationally, through the efforts of their mother and the court.

The Federal Census of 1850 shows that a twenty-one-year-old Lawrence Lafayette Ward was working as a farm hand in Chambers County, Alabama,[1] living in a residence (presumably

1. The county seat of Chambers County happens to be Lafayette, which is

a rooming house) with a number of unrelated people. His ties to Georgia must not have been particularly strong. Despite feeling insecure, he must have developed a strong sense of self-reliance and responsibility for himself and his two younger siblings. Both parents were now dead and he was geographically distant from his older siblings living back in Georgia. His older siblings hardly knew him, since they had grown up and lived in Georgia and L. L. had by this time spent most of his years in Alabama. His maternal grandparents, Webb and Elizabeth Kidd, had died years before L. L. was born.

Grandfather William died in 1850, at age ninety-two, after having been declared an "insane person" (probably suffering from what today would be recognized as age-related dementia) by the recently formed Georgia Lunacy Commission located in Milledgeville, Georgia. Although William had not been in good health for some time before he died, his death came as a blow to L. L. To complete the picture of L. L.'s circumstances in 1850, his paternal grandmother Sarah Vernon Ward had also died years before, in 1840.

With an abiding sense of loss of family (father, mother, grandparents, and separated from most other relatives except for Millie and John), L. L. must have felt very alone in the world. Yet over the years he would have carried with him the memory of his grandfather William, especially the memory of his grandfather's strength of character as conveyed through his wonderful stories. Then there was the positive influence of his own education in Alabama as well as his early formative experiences in Georgia at Van's Creek Baptist Church. This church had been his mother's family church for generations. She would surely have brought him there regularly. The memories and ideals carried from those early years would give him the strength and confidence to move forward from the losses in his life.

That very year, in April 1850, L. L. turned twenty-one, and his fortunes took a turn and changed very much for the better. He began to see his future more clearly now. He met a local girl

---

Lawrence's middle name, the name of a famous Revolutionary War general.

from Chambers County, Lucy Ann Marshall, and on June 19, 1851, they were married by Justice of the Peace Richard Fretwell. Although he was only twenty-two and she only fifteen and a half at the time, her parents, also Baptists, approved of the union and warmly welcomed him into the family. They could see that he was bright, ambitious, a serious man and devout Baptist churchgoer who knew how to work hard, a man capable of supporting a family. He had obtained the essentials of an education. And he was tall and good-looking, possessing a certain confidence, or perhaps even the charisma of a natural leader.

Likewise, Lucy must have been all that L. L. was looking for in a wife: young, healthy, pretty, and obviously smart and capable. She was experienced in helping her mother take care of six younger siblings. Moreover, it certainly didn't hurt that her father, Jesse Marshall, and his wife, Catherine, were originally from Wilkes County, Georgia, located near L. L.'s birthplace in Elbert County.[2] (Lucy had been born in Alabama after the Marshalls moved there.) Truly the Marshalls were not losing a daughter but gaining a son. For his part, this must have been the family he had always dreamed of having. Lucy's father was then in his mid-forties, an age typical for the father of a twenty-two-year-old boy. In contrast, Abner, his deceased biological father, who had abandoned the family when L. L. was five, would have attained the relatively advanced age of sixty-four were he still alive in that year, 1851.

L. L. and the Marshalls were open to the possibility of a future beyond Alabama, in the new state of Texas, sharing the vision of a new life beyond their present one. Later that same year, L. L. and his wife Lucy, along with her mother Catherine, father Jesse, and the younger Marshall children, packed up their belongings into an ox cart and moved across the country to that new life in Upshur County, Texas, to a place that had been part of the United States for only six years. In 1858, seven years after their move to Upshur County in East Texas and just three years before the Civil War would break out in 1861, L. L. and Lucy moved even farther west, to North Central Texas—to the Deep Creek Community in Wise

2. Elbert County was created from Wilkes County in 1790.

County, Texas, where they were to spend the rest of their days. Jesse and Catherine stayed behind in Upshur County, living within reasonable proximity to their daughter, son-in-law, and grandchildren. Besides Lucy Ann and her husband, three other Marshall children and spouses moved to Wise County with them: Mary Ann and husband Richard Boyd, Martha and husband Madison Walker, and bachelor John S. Marshall.

At this time in Texas history, although the Republic of Texas had joined the union in 1846 following its annexation by the United States in 1845, its political future was in doubt. The voters had supported a state constitution that approved of slavery, and this constitution was approved by the U.S. Congress. The approval of slavery as an institution was strongest in the eastern counties of Texas, where Upshur was situated, counties whose prosperity depended heavily upon large cotton-growing plantations worked by slaves. (By 1860, the U.S. Census reported that the population of Upshur had increased to 10,645, including 3,794 slaves.[3]) Farther west, farming was mostly done on small family farms, not on plantations.

Besides the question of slavery in Texas, there was the overshadowing issue of debt owed to the United States, debt accumulated during the ten-year existence of the Republic of Texas (1836–1846). That issue was finally resolved by the Compromise of 1850, which ceded large portions of Texas's western territory to the U.S. in return for forgiveness of the debt. This solidified the state borders and created some years of stability beginning in 1850, eleven years before the Civil War began in 1861, making the state inviting to immigrants from the southeastern U.S. (Texas also welcomed refugees from Europe after the liberating Continental wars of 1848, including those areas that later became Germany and the Czechoslovakia. This multicultural environment created a "live and let live" or libertarian culture still visible in Texas today.)

Although Texas officially joined the Confederacy on the eve of the Civil War, as a whole it was more politically neutral than the Deep South states. It attracted anti-slavery idealists like Lawrence

3. Federal Census, 431 (image 393).

Ward into lesser slave-populated areas like Wise County. "The majority of Wise County settlers were immigrants from southern states, though only fifty-three of the county's 3,160 white residents owned slaves in 1860."[4] Many of the immigrants came to a "Texas [that] in its Wild West days attracted men who could shoot straight and possessed the zest for adventure, 'for masculine renown, patriotic service, martial glory and meaningful deaths.'"[5]

Figure 15. Lawrence Lafayette Ward and Lucy Ann Marshall

Lawrence and Lucy raised their family in a relatively more pro-unionist region, one less economically dependent on the institution of slavery, and there they "did well and made good" as the expression goes. Lawrence L. Ward is recognized today as a pioneer resident of Deep Creek and one of its outstanding citizens. The census of 1880 declares him to be a farmer; however, he assumed many other roles as civic leader and keeper of the peace, including justice of the peace, militia member, and judge, as stated

4. England, "Wise County."
5. Bryan, "Patriot-Warrior." 114.

in the following memorial of the Ward family from a history of Wise County:

> The father, Lawrence L. Ward, was one of the efficient representative citizens of his time. For a number of years he was honored with the office of Justice of the Peace of his precinct, a very responsible position in the early days of the county. Later on Mr. Ward served the county as its Chief Justice, the office of County Judge in the first years of the county organization. When Indian troubles became rife Mr. Ward aligned himself with the Deep Creek militia company, was elected its First Lieutenant, and in this capacity served many years as the defender of the county. His children had the beginnings of their education on Deep Creek under the able tutorship of Robert Walker.[6]

The importance Lawrence Ward attached to education is visible in this memorial, since his children's tutor, Robert Walker, is mentioned by name. L. L. surely never forgot the value of the education that he himself had received from his tutor and guardian back in Shelby County, Alabama, arranged by his mother Franky. He understood education in the expanded sense of formation of the mind and heart of a whole person, within a community that needed protection from destructive forces. This emerged as an important ideal held by the Ward family over several generations, beginning at least with Franky and the Kidd family.[7] L. L. would never forget his youthful experiences at Van's Creek Baptist Church, where his mother and other Kidd relatives had been long-time members.[8] In valuing education and church and community as she did, Franky must have made sure her children had a firm foundation for life under difficult circumstances.

---

6. Cates, *Pioneer History*, 252.

7. Of course, the Ward's Scotch-Irish heritage would have valued formal higher education for Presbyterian ministers, with basic biblical and moral education given to all.

8. Franky and her older siblings William and Elizabeth joined this church in 1802.

In addition to education, Lawrence Lafayette Ward also valued community service, implied by being appointed Wise County Judge and serving as member of the local militia. Here the Ward family ideals of peace keeper and guardian are visible. L. L.'s and Lucy's dedication to the Baptist Church and to education as a public good is also apparent—at least indirectly—from the lives of their children.

The 1880 U.S. Census lists the following members of the Ward household and their ages: Lawrence L. Ward, fifty-one; Lucy A., forty-four; Henry L., twenty-five; William E., nineteen; James F., seventeen; Jesse L., thirteen; and Lucy E., ten.[9] All the sons were said to be "outstanding citizens" of their time as well as active in the Baptist Church. The daughters married solid citizens from the area. Oldest daughter Mary Elizabeth married Mark Oates, a farmer in Wise County, and her sister Lucy Ella married Jefferson Ballard, a minister in Waco. Jesse L. ("J. L.") Ward, was to become a Baptist minister as well as a leader of Christian education in Texas, serving as President of Decatur Baptist College for more than forty years. It is to his story that we turn next.

LAWRENCE LAFAYETTE WARD'S TIMELINE

1829   April 3. Lawrence Lafayette ("L. L.") Ward is born in Elbert County, Georgia.

1837   Father Abner Ward dies intestate when L. L. is eight; mother Frances "Franky" Kidd Ward arranges schooling for L. L. and his two younger siblings in Shelby County, Alabama, their expenses paid through the probate court from the proceeds of Abner's estate.

---

9. The oldest child, daughter Mary Elizabeth Ward, twenty-eight in 1880, was not then living in her parents' home, having been married to Marcus Taylor Oates in 1869.

1850   L. L. works as a farmhand in Chambers County, Alabama. He meets Lucy Ann Marshall and the Marshall family.

1851   L. L. and Lucy are married.

1851   L. L., Lucy, her parents and other members of the Marshall family move from Alabama to Upshur County in East Texas.

1858   L. L. and family move farther west to the Deep Creek Community, Wise County in North Central Texas.

1895   March 21. Lawrence Lafayette Ward dies in Rhome, Wise County, Texas and is buried in Deep Creek Cemetery near Decatur, Wise County, Texas.

6

North Texas 2:
Clerk, Preacher, President

JESSE LAWRENCE ("J. L.") Ward, the youngest of the four sons of L. L. Ward, was born in 1866 at Deep Creek, Wise County, Texas near Decatur, Texas. After finishing public school at age seventeen, he worked as a clerk in a store in Decatur. He married Jennie Beard in 1885 when he was nineteen.

Two years later, J. L. entered into a business partnership with his older brothers. J. L. was then twenty-one. His brothers were Henry, thirty-three; Billy, twenty-six; and Frank, twenty-five. They ran a general merchandise business called Ward Brothers Mercantile, in Springtown, Texas. By all accounts, the business was successful.

However, while working as a clerk at the store and describing himself as feeling "cold and backslidden" after eight years of not going to church, J. L. attended a prayer meeting at a local church. At the meeting, he made a decision to join the church, Springtown Baptist Church. Thereafter, he began to read the Bible in spare moments while working at the store. He began to preach in churches around Springtown.

Five years later, he was ordained and pastoring part-time at churches in Cottondale, Pleasant Grove, Azle, and Aurora during 1892–93. Believing he was being called into full-time Christian ministry, he sold his share in the store partnership and enrolled in Baylor University in 1893. He completed three years of college work at Waco while managing to support himself, a wife, and two small children. However, he was not able to complete all the requirements for a degree. A full-time ministerial opportunity beckoned before he could finish. (Or, as his daughter Elizabeth later observed, maybe his money just ran out.) He was called to be pastor of First Baptist Church, Decatur, Texas.[1]

Figure 16. Jesse Lawrence Ward.

While he was pastoring in Decatur, J. L. was exchanging ideas concerning the future of higher education in Texas with well-connected friends in Waco and in the business world. These exchanges

1. Lasher, *Ministerial Directory*, 763.

culminated in a proposal that the Baptist General Convention of Texas (BGCT) support a new educational institution in Decatur, Decatur Baptist College (DBC).

The school was designed from the beginning to be a junior college, preparing students with varying educational backgrounds for entry into Baylor University, but it was, itself, not offering college degrees. Besides helping to bring the school into existence, J. L. provided institutional leadership as president of its board of trustees during the first two years of the school's existence. Professor B. F. Giles of Howard College, Alabama, was elected as the first president of DBC (1898–1900).

After President Giles resigned in 1900, J. L. was elected by the board to become the second president of Decatur Baptist College, "the world's first junior college," maintaining that position for a total of forty-three years—not counting a hiatus of seven years, 1907–1914—until his retirement in 1950.

The curriculum of the college proposed by J. L. Ward, J. M. Carroll, and others was developed in such a way that work there could be credited as work completed at a four-year institution. The arrangement between DBC and Baylor, the flagship four-year Baptist institution in Texas, provided a model for coordination of the curricula of Baptist schools across the state. A diploma from DBC would qualify the holder for entry into Baylor's junior class. And perhaps even more important, their plan proposed state-wide financial support for the state's Baptist colleges. J. L. Ward's contribution to the advancement of the Baptist higher education system in Texas was in this way visionary and enduring.

Figure 17. Decatur Baptist College administration building.

Numerous stories such as this one have been told of J. L.'s ability to persuade others to enter into projects with him, whether they were persons of means and influence or students barely able to survive financially, to enlist them into a shared vision of their future and then work with them to bring that future to pass. Some might call this ability "salesmanship" or "leadership." Another description that seems applicable to him is "charismatic," meaning, according to one dictionary entry, "exercising a compelling charm which inspires devotion in others."[2]

One thing is certain: he had a deep understanding of human psychology and knew how to apply it. That knowledge served him well as a talented teacher, knowing how and when to be a strict

2. https://www.lexico.com/en/definition/charismatic.

J. L.'s father, Lawrence Lafayette Ward (as well as others in this family), also seemed to possess this kind of personality.

disciplinarian,[3] or patient instructor, or sympathetic friend, or kindly father figure to the students, as the need and occasion arose. This knowledge and ability was rooted in a deep study of the Bible, a love of God, and love for humanity, with a sense of responsibility for those needing his encouragement, guidance, or protection.

And he was always teaching. As Charles "Tom" Gettys later noted, as a preacher "[Ward] was expository . . . And very educational in his preaching. He was not, as Brother Bell [pastor of First Baptist Church, Decatur] was, a loud preacher. He was more of a teacher and explainer." Gettys went on to say:

> Brother Ward was a firm man, he was an excellent disciplinarian, he understood kids—boys and girls. He knew what they were thinking before they thought it. And he knew how to control it. But at the same time, he was a very gentle man and a very pleasing man to be around. Brother Ward was a part not only of the college and the church, but he was equally a part of the community. And when I say community, I'm not talking about just Decatur or Wise County, I'm talking about the community the college reached, all of North Central Texas. He was a highly respected man, very much in demand for weddings and funerals because he was very compassionate.[4]

J. L. Ward would teach a lesson in human psychology and the power of money in a story from his childhood that was later repeated by his youngest daughter, Elizabeth. She recalled:

> His wife would call him Larry. The Jesse was from his grandfather [Jesse] Marshall. And, that was one of father's stories that he would tell. He said, "Every man has a price. We can all be bought. Mortal man can be

3. When an interviewer asked former DBC student, later professor and college dean, Charles "Tom" Gettys, if Ward had mellowed in later years, he answered, "This is true. [But] he realized he had the children of other parents there and he was responsible for them. So he was very strict in the comingling of the boys and girls. It is said there was an invisible fence built across the campus and the boys had to stay on this side and the girls on that side." Charles T. Gettys, unpublished interview, April 10, 1997.

4. Charles T. Gettys, unpublished interview, April 10, 1997.

bought. . . ." Grandfather [Jesse] kept picking at this little kid to say his name was Jesse, and he'd say no, his name was Lawrence. Wasn't Jesse at all. [Grandfather] said, "I'll give you a dime!" And after that, my father would say his name was Jesse.[5]

In regard to J. L.'s attitude toward money as an adult, one observer pointed out that

> Dr. Ward was a thrifty man. He made money, but he enjoyed keeping it more than making it. He was not a generous man with his family, but with his church his generosity was unmatched . . . he always out gave anybody in the church . . . He said that when he was saved he was a covetous person, but the Lord touched his pocketbook as well as his soul.[6]

In regard to relationships, Elizabeth told me that when her father would lead the family in prayer, he would follow the model of the Lord's Prayer in addressing God as "Our Heavenly Father,"[7] showing in that simple way the pattern of a right relationship with God as father and friend, neither as stern judge nor as best buddy.

J. L. had an ability to easily establish relationships with others, even strangers, as if they were trusted friends, approaching them with humility, disarming them of their fears or hesitations. He had even greater confidence in his friends.[8]

A story illustrates J. L. Ward's power to inspire, motivate, and explain to others how to live authentically in the face of difficulties, while at the same time respecting the individuals' freedom to

5. Elizabeth Ann Ward Robertson, unpublished interview by Charles T. Gettys, October 6, 1994.

6. Esther Watkins, "I Knew Dr. Ward," unpublished interview, November 15, 1973.

7. Elizabeth Ann Ward Robertson, private communication with author at DBC's 100th Anniversary Alumni Reunion, Decatur, Texas, 1998.

8. Esther Watkins, "I Knew Dr. Ward." "His having confidence in his friends was almost a fault. When he was convinced of a person's friendship and loyalty, that individual could 'get by' with anything. Since he was truthful and honest, he just supposed other people were too; especially did he feel that way about all his friends."

choose as independent moral agents. A new student at Decatur Baptist College, W. W. Melton (later a leader in the denomination), became discouraged and was ready to drop out of school. As Melton later related events, after the president had learned of his intentions,

> Ward went with [me to my] room, closed the door and bolted it. Then, drawing a chair close . . . he sat beside me and, in a most confidential and brotherly spirit, he said, "Tell me what has happened. I am your friend and I want to help you." [I] told him what had happened. Then [he] said something that was the turning point in [my] life. Ward began to talk.
>
> He did not scold me nor did he beg me to remain in school. But for an hour he talked plain, practical, common sense things about what it meant to live, to live well, to live nobly, to live on a high plane, to live for a purpose, to live so that one's life would be a blessing to the world. I had never thought of life like that before, nor did I know so many things could be said about life. The longer he talked, the meaner I felt. My head got down between my knees. I could not look up. . . . After about an hour he arose and he put out his hand to tell me good-bye and said, "What are you going to do?" I told him I was going to stay until I learned everything they could teach me.[9]

J. L.'s first period as president of DBC (1900–1907) was interrupted by the unexpected death of his wife Jennie Beard, who had served as matron of the college dormitories. This event led to his resignation. He moved to Waco to serve as secretary to the Baptist State Educational Commission (1907–1908). This was followed by a return to pastoral work.

However, in 1914 he was again named president, remarried the following year to Elizabeth "Lizzie" Penn Dickson, and remained as president of DBC until his final resignation in 1950. (At the time of their marriage, Lizzie was a widow. She became the school dietitian and was "greatly loved by the students,"[10] while

9. Melton, *Stories*, 108–10.
10. Williams, *To God Be the Glory*, 28.

also assisting J. L. in the ordering of his daily affairs at school and at home.)

In 1927, J. L. publicly debated Fort Worth Fundamentalist Baptist J. Frank Norris and former DBC student John R. Rice (editor of the weekly *The Sword of the Lord*), in defense of a moderate, mainstream Southern Baptist position, against attack from a Fundamentalist Baptist position. Theologically, J. L. was a "postmillennialist," while the Fundamentalists espoused "premillennialism."[11]

Politically, Jesse Lawrence Ward was a member of the Democratic Party (at that time, that meant a Southern Conservative), a strong supporter of individuals' and states' rights, and against external intervention, especially military intervention. He was a strong advocate of personal morality, self-discipline, and freedom from debt and from personal vices such as drinking and gambling. While he was very much an Evangelical Christian, he was also something of an Enlightenment idealist, numbering himself among the Freemasons, who were advocates of a liberal ideal of freedom through education (if not for an orthodox view of God). That may have been one reason he was an advocate for a foundational, classical education for his students at DBC. However, his purpose in education was always to build strong Christians who would be useful citizens of the church *and of the community*, made fit for all manner of good work.

Admittedly, J. L. had a tendency to take himself and his reputation (or public image) too seriously. This could be expressed as an excessive confidence in his own ability to solve problems, including mechanical problems, a confidence that was not necessarily based on God-gifted ability in such matters.

A story has been told of his attempt to fix a broken windmill on the DBC campus after someone else had failed. Apparently, he presented an astonishing sight to onlookers as he climbed the windmill tower dressed in his good clothes (including his starched white shirt and tie and wearing a Prince Albert coat), fell into the

---

11. The Fundamentalists' premillennial view maintained that Christ's second coming will be immediately followed by Christ's thousand-year reign on Earth.

water trough, and climbed out looking thoroughly disheveled, "madder than a wet hen." The sight provoked an amused reaction by his daughter, after he had "stalked away." Clearly embarrassed, he would have had to explain the poor state of his clothing to his wife Lizzie, upon whom he had come to depend to order his daily attire. If clothes didn't *make* the man, they certainly were crucial to maintain the *image* of a man concerned with his reputation as a figure of authority in Decatur.

After personal integrity, reputation was clearly an important ideal for J. L. Ward as it was for the college. He maintained a well-deserved reputation for fiscal conservatism, working tirelessly to decrease the debt of DBC. Being (mostly) free of debt proved essential for financial survival of the college during the lean years of the Great Depression. However, "in the 1930–1931 academic year, [when] the college was forced to assume additional debt . . . at times, only Ward's good name kept the college afloat."[12] Although he never earned a college degree, J. L. Ward's achievements were recognized by his being awarded two honorary degrees, the MA from Baylor University and the DD from Hardin-Simmons University.

Jesse Lawrence Ward helped so many, and was beloved by so many, yet he was humanly vulnerable to disappointment when others did not live up to his lofty personal standards. Years of unselfish service and financial generosity in the face of so many hardships turned into long-suffering self-sacrifice. Self-sacrifice, when others were seemingly less committed than he, led to internal conflict with his ideal of self-respect. Over the years, he had become so identified with the institution and took such personal responsibility for its order, discipline, finances, and spiritual life, and everything else going on at the school, that the weight of this responsibility took its toll in bitterness that DCB had not received the kind of support from the BGCT that other institutions had, support worthy of the steady financial stewardship of a Jesse Lawrence Ward.[13]

12. Williams, *To God Be the Glory*, 53.

13. For example, Williams, *To God Be the Glory*, 31: "[H]e blamed the lower

Years later, in 1965, after Decatur Baptist College had moved to Dallas and become Dallas Baptist University, a journalist dubbed the students' experience in Decatur under the Ward administration a "benevolent Christian despotism,"[14] recognizing by this provocative expression that transformative education meant bending the whole person, shaping the heart and mind and soul of a person, into a disciplined way of being and becoming, that, for J. L. Ward, was necessary for participating in the fullness of life in Christ, a distinctive way of flourishing in this world and the next. And this way meant being a good citizen of the world, not just following the rules of conventional (Christian) morality, on one's way to heaven.

JESSE LAWRENCE WARD'S TIMELINE

1866	September 24. Jesse Lawrence ("Lawrence," "J. L.") Ward is born in the Deep Creek Community, Wise County, Texas.
1885	January 11. J. L. marries Jennie Beard.
1885	September. Daughter Pearl Joyce Ward is born in Decatur, Texas.
1885–93	J. L. works as a store clerk and preaches in local area churches around Springtown, Texas.
1891	February. Daughter Ruth Lorene Ward is born in Decatur, Texas.
1893	J. L. enters Baylor University. Completes his work there in three years but without receiving a college degree.

---

enrollment [in 1927] on a lack of confidence in the long-term commitment of the BGCT to junior colleges. Ward stated, 'The people in our territory seem to have the impression that the convention will abandon junior colleges as denominational institutions. We will suffer until this impression is removed.'"

14. Porterfield, "Brother Ward."

1896	J. L. Ward accepts a call to become pastor of First Baptist Church, Decatur, Texas.
1897	With J. M. Carroll and others, J. L. Ward formulates a plan to purchase the Decatur property of a defunct college, Northwest Texas College, "on favorable terms"; approval of the plan given by the Baptist General Convention of Texas (BGCT).
1898	September 20. Charter filed for Decatur Baptist College. J. L. is named president of its board of trustees.
1900	J. L. Ward is elected president of Decatur Baptist College.
1907	February 20. Wife Jennie Beard dies. J. L. soon thereafter resigns from presidency of DBC.
1907–08	J. L. Ward, secretary of the Texas Baptist Educational Commission, Waco, Texas.
1908	J. L. becomes pastor of Central Baptist Church, Itasca, Texas.
1910	J. L. becomes pastor of Decatur Baptist Church.
1914	J. L. Ward returns as president of Decatur Baptist College.
1915	J. L. marries Elizabeth Penn Dickson.
1950	J. L. resigns as president of DBC after a total of forty-three years in that position.
1952	July 3. Dr. Jesse Lawrence Ward dies in Decatur and is buried in Deep Creek Cemetery, Boyd, Wise County, Texas.

WILLIAM EDWARD WARD

William E. "Billy" Ward, the second oldest of L. L. Ward's sons, joined his brothers in their business, Ward Brothers Mercantile, located in Wise County, Texas. His life and career were not long lasting, however, as both he, his wife, Tabitha Clementine "Clemmie" Paschall, and a one-year-old infant child named Roy died during the year of 1893, the year Billy turned thirty-two. They died most likely from a contagious disease such as spotted fever or scarlet fever. The couple left behind three children, the oldest being Julian Elvis Ward, age eight. The younger siblings were Edward F. "Ed" Ward, age six, and Nell Clementine Ward, age three.

The orphaned children lived with Julian's maternal grandmother Paschall and, perhaps for a time, with their Uncle Lawrence Ward.

Not much is known of Billy or Clemmie. The Ward story we follow continues with that of their son Julian.

WILLIAM E. WARD'S TIMELINE

1861   January 23. William Edward "Billy" Ward is born in Deep Creek, Wise County, Texas.

1884   January 20. Billy marries Tabitha Clementine "Clemmie" Paschall.

1885   June 11. Son Julian Elvis Ward is born in Rhome, Wise County, Texas.

1887   June 25. Son Edward Francis Ward is born.

1889   March 30. Daughter Nellie Clementine Ward is born.

1891   June 20. Son Roy P. Ward is born.

1893   December 27. William Edward Ward dies at age thirty-two in Rhome, Wise County, Texas. His wife, Clemmie, and infant son, Roy, die the same year.

7

West Texas, California and Beyond

JULIAN ELVIS WARD SR. AND HENRY ELIJAH "HENRIETTA" BROTHERS

JULIAN ELVIS WARD was born in 1885 in Rhome, Wise County, Texas, son of William Edward "Billy" Ward and Tabitha Clementine "Clemmie" Ward. At the age of eight, Julian became an orphan after both of his parents died the same year. He became the oldest of three surviving children.[1] This situation strangely paralleled that of Julian's grandfather, L. L. Ward, who had himself been eight years old with two younger siblings at the time that *his* father died back in Georgia.

In addition to being orphaned, neither of Julian's grandfathers were available to him for long as a source of stability or inspiration

---

1. Near the time of his parents' death (probably from spotted fever or scarlet fever), public health records show an epidemic of spotted fever had been reported in nearby Springtown, Texas (1891). See *Weekly Abstracts*, 66 (from February 13, 1891). Julian's younger siblings were Edward Francis Ward (1887–1952) and Nell Clementine Ward (1889–1964). A younger brother Roy (1891–1893) died in infancy.

in his life: they both died the same year, in 1895, which was just two years after Julian's parents died. So without older siblings, parents, or grandfathers to follow as examples, Julian naturally looked up to his Ward uncles, Henry, Frank, and especially to the youngest, J. L., as father figures for most of his growing-up and young adult years. (J. L., known to him as "Uncle Lawrence," was only nineteen years older than Julian but managed to outlive him by two years.)

The children went to live with their maternal grandparents, Lunsford and Tabitha Frances "Fannie" Paschall, after their parents died in 1893. The U.S. Census of 1900 shows the children living with their by-then-widowed grandmother in Wise County near Deep Creek.

For his part, Uncle Lawrence must have felt a fatherly affection for his nephew, especially since J. L. and Jennie had no son of their own. However, they did have two daughters named Bessie and Ruth, the older one, Bessie, just the same age as Julian. Julian and his younger siblings may have at some point lived with this uncle in his home in Decatur.

Julian attended Decatur Baptist College, the secondary and post-secondary institution where Uncle Lawrence was president, completing the equivalent of four years of high school. He did not pursue higher-level academic work. He married a local school teacher named Henrietta Brothers a few days before his twenty-fifth birthday in 1910, after which the couple visited Galveston, Texas on their honeymoon. (Galveston was the site of the Great Galveston Hurricane in 1900 that had killed eight thousand people.)

The final year of World War I, 1918, found Julian, then age thirty-three and married with a wife and two young children—a boy and a girl, ages six and three, respectively—living seventy-five miles northwest of Decatur, in Wichita Falls, Texas. No disqualifying physical problems were noted on Julian's WWI draft registration form. He was described as "tall, of medium build, 6' 195 lbs." However, being the sole breadwinner of the family as well as constitutionally opposed to the military services, he did not enlist and was not drafted. Julian worked as a station manager for the Western Oil Company in town.

Grandmother Fannie Paschall, who had taken Julian and his siblings in when they were orphaned, in her later years lived with the Wards in Wichita Falls until her death in 1917. Also living with them in 1920 were Julian's unmarried cousins, Henry G. "Grady" Ward (age thirty) and Grady's younger brother Frank T. Ward (age twenty-one), sons of Julian's oldest uncle, Henry L. Ward. Both cousins also worked for the Western Oil Company.

On his draft registration form, Julian described himself as "self-employed as a gasoline & lubricating oil salesman." According to census data in 1920, he described himself simply as employed in the "oil business"; in 1926 he said he was co-owner of Ward & Ramey Filling Station; in 1930—after the family had moved to West Texas the previous year—he described himself as a "self-employed real estate salesman"; and in 1940 he was simply a "salesman" or a "traveling salesman."

Julian was good-looking, charming, and persuasive, blessed with a natural sales personality, in possession of what might be called a healthy ego, holding to definite opinions about politics, religion, and, especially, the importance of the individual to think for him- or herself.

Julian, along with many others in America, suffered through times of "boom and bust" during the 1920s and 1930s (the years of the Great Depression). At one point during those early years, Julian and Henrietta thought they might become wealthy from a certain business investment in the oil business. (Henrietta, many years later, told me with some regret that she had vetoed the investment as too risky.) As it was, the family was one of modest means. They moved to Lubbock in 1929 to enable son Frank and daughter Winnelle to take advantage of the recently opened Texas Technological College.[2] Julian owned and operated an auto parts business in Lubbock and dabbled in real estate while Henrietta

2. Texas Technological College (now Texas Tech University) opened its doors on October 1, 1925. Tuition was affordable for many students struggling financially during the difficult times of the Great Depression (1929–1939).

managed a boarding house at 2101 Thirteenth Street, where they lived upstairs.

Julian travelled extensively due to his work as a salesman, travel that would take him west to California and, according to family lore, as far as Seattle, Washington. During his business trips, he would certainly have visited his favorite cousin, Grady Ward, who had relocated to Oakland, California from Wichita Falls sometime in the early 1920s. (The thirty-eight-year-old bachelor Grady married thirty-one-year-old Frances A. "Annette" Keene in 1927. Like Grady, she was a transplant from Texas to the California Bay Area. This was her second marriage.)

Julian was known as a strong advocate for self-reliance and state's rights, deeply distrustful of the federal government, especially distrustful of its promises to provide for people's needs (whether for work or for welfare) and of its military actions. He did not approve of his older son's participation in the Boy Scouts, for instance, calling it a form of "regimentation." Nevertheless, while he never joined the armed forces, he would live to see both of his sons serve in the military, during and after World War II. Julian died of a heart attack at the relatively young age of sixty-four in the early morning hours of January 2, 1950, a Monday, just after the New Year's holiday.

Julian's wife, who had been given the name Henry Elijah Brothers at birth (but understandably preferring to be known simply as "Henrietta" or "Etta"), was a native of Weatherford, Parker County, Texas, brought up in the Methodist Church there, and was well known in Methodist and, later, in Baptist circles, as an adult Sunday school teacher in Wichita Falls and Lubbock, Texas. Her early schooling and training in a "normal" school (a two-year post-secondary school for training teachers) prepared her for a teaching career, but she never attended a four-year college. She was smart, attractive, and high-spirited, much sought after by the young men of the area. Her birth name did not seem much of a hindrance, reflecting as it did the early expectations of her father, named—you guessed it—Henry Elijah Brothers.

After a short career as a public school teacher in the vicinity of Parker County, she married a handsome local bachelor named Julian Ward in 1910. Within five years they had two children. Although Henrietta gave up her teaching career to become a homemaker, she was able to continue teaching at home: instructing the children in Latin and in the Bible. Years later, when she was busy running the boarding house, she feared she might neglect her younger son, Julian Jr. (born 1927), and so she hired a young woman staying at the rooming house, Ruby Tom Rhodes, to read to him. Education was important—very important—to Henrietta, as was travel and adventure. She always regretted missing out on a college education.

Henrietta made sure that all three of her children went as far as they could, educationally. As it turned out, all three not only received college degrees, they all pursued post-graduate college or professional training. They had had a head start in academics thanks to their mother. She was strongly ambitious for each of them. They all felt the weight of her ambition for them, a weight which was at times overbearing, in different ways.

Henrietta was a devout Christian, a self-taught Bible scholar, and a popular adult Sunday school teacher. (It is thought by many that she would have made a "powerful" preacher if women had been allowed to serve in that role in the Baptist Church. Since that path was not available, the classroom podium could substitute for a pulpit.) She was smart and highly opinionated about almost everything. She, like Julian, had a healthy ego. Unsurprisingly, their egos did not always see eye to eye (or should that be "I" to "I"?). But the two managed to work as a team; in particular, they were aligned when it came to furthering their children's educations.

She was also known locally as a shrewd businesswoman, a trader, effectively running the Lubbock boarding house for many years, making it a profitable enough enterprise to support the family and put two sons through medical school. She was comfortable being in control of her life and, often, being in control of others' lives. The rules of the boarding house, especially the rules prohibiting alcohol consumption and inappropriate visitation, were strictly enforced. This arrangement was acceptable to her husband, who eventually retired to life at the boarding house.[3]

Figure 18. Julian Elvis Ward Sr. and Henrietta Brothers.

JULIAN E. WARD SR. AND HENRIETTA E. BROTHERS'S TIMELINE

[ ] indicates possible time/event

1885   June 11. Julian Elvis Ward is born in Rhome, Wise County, Texas.

1890   April 24. Henry Elijah "Henrietta" Brothers is born in Weatherford, Parker County, Texas.

3. As reported to me by his son-in-law, William Nelle. Julian may have suffered from heart disease, as he died from a heart attack not long after retirement.

1893	Julian is orphaned at age eight when both his parents die the same year.
1910	June 1. Julian and Henrietta are married in Weatherford.
1912	January 18. Son James Franklin "Frank" Ward is born in Weatherford.
1915	January 28. Daughter Hildred Winnelle Ward is born in Rhome, Wise County, Texas.
[1916]	The Wards relocate to Wichita Falls, Texas.
1917	January 15. Fannie Paschall, Julian's grandmother living with them, dies.
1927	March 15. Son Julian Elvis Jr. "Julian" Ward is born in Wichita Falls.
1929	Julian, Henrietta, and family move to Lubbock, Texas with the intention that Frank (and Winnelle) will attend the new college there, established four years earlier. They operate a boarding house at 2101 Thirteenth Street, near the new campus of Texas Technological College, feeding many students and faculty during dark days of the Great Depression.
1950	January 2. Julian dies of a heart attack in Lubbock, Texas. He is buried in Resthaven Cemetery.
1983	September 14. Henrietta dies in Lubbock, Texas. She is also buried in Resthaven Cemetery.

Henrietta's obituary was matter-of-fact, listing her involvement with numerous social clubs as well as church, Sunday school, and Bible study activities. What it failed to mention was her influence on many persons, not just on those in her family or church members, and her life as an inspired teacher, Christian evangelist, counselor, and friend to many. It failed to mention her business acumen. It also failed to mention her extensive world travels in later life, including trips to visit family members living in Europe or her round-the-world trip with a granddaughter, Marion Ruth

Ward, after her husband's death. She also made other gifts of travel experiences to her grandchildren, particularly if she thought that the investment might enrich their educational or religious development. She proudly displayed on a shelf in her living room a picture of herself perched on the back of a camel in the North African desert, Egyptian pyramids visible in the distance.

The following notice appeared in the *Lubbock Avalanche-Journal* after her death in 1983:

> Services for Henrietta Ward, 93, of 1717 Norfolk Ave. are pending with Rix Funeral Directors. She died at 2:15 p.m. Sunday at Methodist Hospital. Born April 24, 1890, in Parker County, she married Julian E. Ward in 1910 at Weatherford. He died in 1950. The couple moved to Lubbock in 1929. Mrs. Ward was a member of First Baptist Church and of the Order of the Eastern Star, the Lubbock Women's Study Club, the Hattie Stallings Circle, the Faith Sunday School Class, Friday Needle Club, Merry Bidders 42 Club and the Llano Estacado Travel-Study Club. A son, Major Julian E. Ward Jr., died in 1962. Survivors include a daughter, Mrs. William H. (Winnelle) Nelle of Laramie, Wyo.; a son, Dr. James Frank Ward, of Tacoma, Wash.; a sister, Hildred Shorten of Weatherford; a brother, T. Lawrence Brothers, of Cresson; 11 grandchildren; and eight great-grandchildren. The family suggests memorials be made to the American Bible Society.

JAMES F. WARD SR., MD

Julian and Henrietta's oldest son, James Franklin "Frank" Ward Sr., MD, was a remarkable man of accomplishment. Early in life, he was recognized as a history scholar: at age nineteen he wrote a college master's thesis on post-revolutionary Russian experiments in education. Five years later, he taught high school history in Lubbock, then served on teams doing archeological research in the Southwest and Mexico with professors and students from Texas Tech. He was also a social worker in the Bay Area of California, a medical student at Baylor College of Medicine, graduate of

Harvard Medical School, WWII veteran, and resident in eye surgery at the University of Pennsylvania.

For many years he maintained a private medical practice in Tacoma, Washington. In the early 1950s he led a pioneering Great Books Program study and discussion group in Tacoma, collected historical gold coins, and played chess with a few intimate friends. He read widely and occasionally lectured at a local coin club. He was at one time a member of the local Unitarian-Universalist Church, a 32nd Degree Mason, and member of the Tacoma Elks Club. He was also a respected ophthalmologist and well-known eccentric in the Tacoma area.

He once related to me a visit he had made as a boy to the farm of his maternal grandparents (Henry Elijah Brothers and Mannassah Davis Smith) in Parker County, Texas. He was proud of their life of self-sufficiency and independence, proud that they could make or grow anything they needed to live—except for sugar and coffee. He was taught Bible and Latin at home by his mother while growing up in Wichita Falls. As a young man, he joined the Baptist Church and taught Sunday school there.

Figure 19. James F. Ward Sr., MD, c. 1943

During the Great Depression days of the early 1930s, as a teenager he would help the family stay afloat financially by selling fireworks by the roadside. He also did heavy physical labor, including hauling bricks from an abandoned schoolhouse in Matador, Texas to Lubbock to provide material to build an apartment house, located on Broadway one block east of the Texas Tech campus. Rental of the apartment units supplemented income from the boarding house his mother ran on Thirteenth Street. By all accounts, he was a serious, talented, and hard-working person. He was also highly ambitious and driven to succeed, handsome and aware that he possessed a certain persuasive, charismatic power like certain other

Ward family members. As is true of people with well-developed egos, he had friends and supporters; there were others, however, who were not exactly fans.

Unfortunately, Frank developed health problems, including what might be today diagnosed as depression, social phobia, or mania.[4] These problems were extremely disruptive of his family and work life. His life was one of promise and accomplishment but, sadly, a life that in later years went "off the rails."

While definite indications of these problems emerged in his forties, he *may* have exhibited signs of difficulties earlier in life. His mother related to me that when he was in grade school, she was called to the school by school officials after an incident in which he allegedly attacked (or, according to him, defended himself from being attacked by) a group of boys on a playground who had surrounded him in a threatening way. He was accused of using a pocketknife as a weapon. No other details of the incident were provided, but it is clear from the mother's account of it to me that this episode became a public embarrassment.

Frank's self-admitted penchant for bragging, for showing off his encyclopedic knowledge, for thrill-seeking adventures, including driving cars at high speeds and riding in fast aircraft, was perhaps related to these health issues. In fairness, it might be argued that at least the first of these traits seems to be commonly observed in Texan culture and shared by other members of the Ward family.

Frank was involved in a public scandal that took place in California and Texas during his early adult life. It involved an alleged kidnapping following a custody battle for his young daughter. This was reported from sources in San Franciso to the local Lubbock, Texas newspaper, on Friday, August 11, 1939, when Frank was twenty-seven (his age was misstated in the article) and recently divorced from his first wife, Frances Simmons:[5]

4. I am not professionally qualified to make such a determination. I am simply stating common beliefs within the family.

5. Frances Loraine Simmons, b. August 20, 1916, in Hico, Hamilton, Texas; d. November 17, 1994, in Sweeny, Brazoria, Texas.

San Francisco, Aug. 10, 1939. Inspector Frank Lucey said tonight the reported theft of two-year-old Sonia Louise Ward from a San Francisco parish home was proved a hoax when two women who reported the incident confessed to the deception. A child stealing charge and an order to pick up James Ward, 29, of Lubbock, Texas, father of the girl, were cancelled by police.

Had Signed Complaint. Inspector Lucey said Mrs. Frances Ward, the child's mother, admitted the child had not been with her for more than a year, but instead was in Texas with Ward, from whom she was divorced in Monterey County in June, 1937. He said the woman's longing to have the child back apparently had resulted in the hoax. Mrs. Ward and a housekeeper had told officers a tall, dark man came to the door of their home, the parish house of the Rev. Constantino Tsapralis Wednesday night and snatched the child from the arms of the housekeeper. The housekeeper said she concurred in the story to "please" Mrs. Ward. Inspector Lucey said no action probably would be taken against the women. Mrs. Ward had signed the child stealing warrant against Ward.

Custody of Child Contested Over Period of Many Months. Parental custody of two-year-old Sonia Louise Ward, daughter of Mr. and Mrs. James Franklin Ward, formerly of Lubbock, has been contested several months, relatives here said Thursday. Ward, who taught history in Senor High school one term three years ago, is the son of Mrs. J. E. Ward, who operates a boarding house at 2101 Thirteenth Street. The mother is now in California, friends said. Mrs. Ward is the daughter of Mr. and Mrs. J. W. Simmons, 2223 Tenth Street.

Married In Clovis. James Franklin Ward and the then Miss Frances Simmons were married in Clovis three years ago last February, her parents related this morning. Miss Simmons, they added, was a dietician, a work in which she was engaged part of the time while with her husband and since their separation. "My daughter has been trying to find that baby for more than a year—ever since the court in California gave her custody of the child," Mrs. Simmons related this morning.

This scandal, with its disruption of social and family life, should not obscure Frank's many accomplishments. These were achieved against the challenges of the Great Depression, World War II, and difficulties faced in his younger years, including the struggle for independence from an overbearing mother, divorce from his first wife, completing medical school, wartime service as a medic in the South Pacific (in the trenches of Iwo Jima), and the burden of supporting a family of six children (not including the daughter from his first marriage). The death of his father in 1950 and younger brother in 1962 were devastating blows.

While working for many years as an ophthalmologist in Tacoma, Frank took special pride in leading a Great Books Program[6] study and discussion group in the early 1950s, at that time a pioneering effort in the Northwestern U.S.[7] This avocation revealed what might have been his true vocation, that of professor, lecturer, and generalist in the humanities. As he later told me, he turned from the humanities to the medical field at the suggestion of a

6. This was based on the Great Books of the Western World, a library started by academics in the 1920s and 1930s. The library was initiated by Prof. John Erskine of Columbia University and intended to return education to the Western liberal arts tradition of broad cross-disciplinary learning. The Great Books Program was designed to make reading and discussion of the classics available to all.

7. These discussion groups provided a platform to work out his personal philosophical, religious, and political views; in particular, he found his way toward acceptance of new traditions, from the East and West, moving away from his Baptist heritage.

Frank was an admirer of German philosopher Arthur Schopenhauer and his system of "metaphysical volunteerism." For Schopenhauer, the will is the "sole truly real, primary, metaphysical thing in a world in which everything else is only appearance" (*On the Will in Nature*). Thus "human desire [is] futile, illogical, directionless, and, by extension, so [is] all human action in the world" (https://en.wikipedia.org/wiki/Arthur_Schopenhauer). This view contradicts that of Jonathan Edwards in his *Freedom of the Will*. For Edwards, we have freedom (of our "natural will") to will what we want even if the "moral will" has been corrupted by our sinful nature. Freedom of the will was important to the first generation of Wards who became Baptists.

colleague (associated with the archeological teams he had worked on in the early 1930s). The suggestion was that medical training would provide a solid foundation for a career in physical anthropology. This career aspiration was sidetracked first of all due to the demands of wartime—he graduated from medical school at the height of the war in 1943. After the war, he realized that a growing family would require the financial stability provided by a medical practice rather than an academic appointment in the humanities.

And so medical school and wartime service were followed by three years of specialty medical training in ophthalmology at the University of Pennsylvania. He chose to specialize in the surgical treatment of eye diseases. The eye held a special fascination for him as an ancient symbol of esoteric knowledge and wisdom. He often mentioned that he wanted the Egyptian "Eye of Horus" motif to decorate the waiting room of his future clinic.

Sadly, the health problems mentioned earlier intervened and made sustaining the medical practice difficult. He stopped performing eye surgery and eventually limited his practice to office consultations, toward the end of his career accepting only children as new patients. He ran a small but successful side business dispensing optical products, prescription lenses, and frames.

James Franklin Ward Sr. died in Tacoma in September 1988, age seventy-six. The cause of death was attributed to a type of liver cancer related to alcoholism.

JAMES F. WARD, SR. MD'S TIMELINE

[ ] indicates possible time/event

1912	January 18. James Franklin Ward Sr. is born in Weatherford, Parker County, Texas.
1915	January 28. Sister Hildred Winnelle Ward is born in Rhome, Wise County, Texas.
[1916]	Frank moves with his parents, sister, and great grandmother to Wichita Falls, Texas.

1929	The family moves to Lubbock from Wichita Falls.
1931	Frank graduates from Texas Technological College, receiving simultaneously two degrees: BA and MA (history).
1936	Frank teaches history for one term at Tom S. Lubbock High School. He also serves as volunteer member on Texas Tech archeological teams doing research excavations in Mexico and other parts of the Southwest.
1936	February. Marries Frances Louise Simmons in Clovis, New Mexico.
1937	May 29. Daughter Sonia Louise is born.
1937	June. Frank divorces Frances in Monterey, California.
[1937–39]	Frank is employed as a social worker in Berkeley, California. He takes premed classes at UC Berkeley.
1939	Frank enters Baylor College of Medicine, Dallas, Texas.
1941	June 13. Frank marries second wife Rubye Katherine Hutchings (secretly) in Rockwall, Texas, contrary to Baylor Nursing School rules.
1941	Frank transfers into the third-year class of Harvard Medical School, Boston, Massachusetts.
1943	Frank graduates from Harvard Medical School and enlists immediately with the Navy/Marines for medical combat duty in the South Pacific.
1945	May 22. James Franklin Ward Jr. is born in San Diego, California.
1946	July 29. Katherine Winnelle Ward is born in San Diego, California.
1947	Frank is discharged from military duty.

1947–50	Frank assumes residency in ophthalmology at the University of Pennsylvania/Wills Eye Hospital, Philadelphia.
1949	November 15. Marion Ruth Ward is born in Philadelphia.
1950	Frank and family move to the Seattle area (first to an apartment in the city, then to private residence in Bellevue). He joins a group ophthalmology practice in Seattle, then opens his own office in Tacoma.
1951	April 4. William Grady Ward is born in Seattle, Washington.
1952	The family moves from the Seattle suburb of Bellevue to 622 North 4th Street, Tacoma, Washington.
1953.	November 25. Susan Lorelle Ward is born in Tacoma, Washington.
1958	March 4. Ann Lynne Ward is born in Tacoma, Washington.
1988	September 10. James F. Ward Sr. dies in Tacoma, Washington.
2007	June 30. Rubye Katherine Hutchings Ward dies in Tacoma, Washington.

HILDRED WINNELLE WARD NELLE

Frank's sister, Hildred "Winnelle" Ward, was born in 1915 in Rhome, Wise County, Texas three years after Frank. Having spent most of her earlier years in Wichita Falls, Texas, she moved with her family to Lubbock in 1929, where she was graduated from Lubbock High School in 1931. She was a precocious student like her brother. Her high school senior-year picture reveals a serious-looking, attractive sixteen-year-old whose extracurricular activities included Latin Club, music, and "Pep Squad." She excelled both academically and socially.

Winnelle enrolled at Texas Tech University in 1931. Her daughter, Julia Vandine, reported to me that "[in those practical-minded Great Depression days] she was told by her parents she *would* attend [Texas Tech] and *would* major in Home Economics with a Clothing Construction minor [emphases added]."[8]

During her student years at Tech, she waited on tables at the boarding house at 2101 13th Street, Lubbock, Texas. This is where she met her future husband, William Haden Nelle, also a student at Texas Tech in 1931. Winnelle "courted William Nelle but dated others until 1934. At that time he chased her around a picnic table at Carlsbad Caverns, New Mexico and proposed to her."

On one occasion in the mid-1930s, William, Winnelle, and several students from Tech (including her older brother, Frank) "went on a Mexican adventure with William Holden (a Texas Tech history and archeology professor), driving old cars on narrow dirt roads [that] turned to mud in the rain forests."

While Winnelle was still a college student, before she and her husband-to-be were married, William Nelle sold auto parts for her father, Julian E. Ward Sr. After Winnelle graduated in 1935, William and Winnelle were married in the living room of the boarding house. Accounts of the wedding appeared in a local newspaper.

Following their marriage, Winnelle and William moved to Berkeley, California. "Her parents drove [them there in] a car loaded down with all [the young couple's] worldly possessions. The parents . . . were very large people. William and Winnelle were very thin! What a picture they [presented to the couple's new] neighbors, who became [their] life-long friends." The parents then returned to Texas, leaving Winnelle and William to find their way in California.

Winnelle applied her talent for salesmanship with help from her training in home economics. As her daughter related,

> she sold pancake mixes in grocery stores and later millinery at I. Magnin [from] the [beginning of their time] in California. William was a teaching assistant at the

8. All quotations in this section are from Julia Nelle Vandine in conversation with the author.

University of California, Berkeley. During their time there, Winnelle did post-graduate work in psychology, normal and abnormal, and in child development. After her classes, she applied for and was hired as a social worker for the Alameda County California Welfare Department. She worked there for about 11 years until the birth of her daughter in 1946.

The Nelles moved to Laramie late in 1946. William accepted a position as assistant professor at the University of Wyoming.[9] Winnelle was a stay-at-home mother for several years. She obtained a dealer's license to sell sewing machines, and therefore was able to buy furniture at a discounted rate in Denver furniture warehouses.

While both were working in other jobs, William and Winnelle managed rental properties in Laramie, Wyoming. After they both had retired in 1983, they moved to a new residence at a retirement village in Lubbock. Winnelle died just a few years later, in 1989, from complications of Crohn's disease. A few years after that, William moved to Tacoma, Washington. He was a long-time friend and companion to Rubye K. Ward, widow of James F. Ward Sr. William ded in Tacoma in 1998.

Following the example of her mother and other family members, Winnelle was socially active in a variety of organizations, including the Faculty Women's Club, Sewing Club, the Methodist Church, and the Zonta Club International, a women's service organization. The state of Wyoming presented her an award for outstanding service. As mentioned earlier, she followed her parents' activities in real estate and property management.

9. William completed his PhD at the University of Nebraska, eventually becoming head of the foreign language department at the University of Wyoming.

Figure 20. Winnelle Ward Nelle, social worker.

Growing up in Lubbock, Texas, Winnelle was popular and always had many friends. Like her mother, she was an upbeat and high-spirited person. Like her brothers, she was academically talented, graduating from high school at age sixteen and entering college the same year. Like her older brother, she was employed as a social worker. Also, following her husband, William, and brother Frank, she was sympathetic to "left-leaning" social and political causes. She exemplified many of the Ward family ideals, which included greatly valuing education, skillfully applying human psychology (being influential, having a natural sales personality), and making use of a practical business sense while seeking adventure and travel.

Being authentic in the family tradition meant helping others by protecting and enlightening them. Winnelle gained self-fulfillment in this way partly through her roles of mother and social worker. It also meant being enterprising when the need and opportunity arose.

HILDRED WINNELLE WARD NELLE'S TIMELINE

[ ] indicates possible time/event

1915   January 28. H. Winnelle Ward is born in Rhome, Texas.

[1916]   Winnelle moves with her parents and older brother to Wichita Falls, Texas.

1929   She moves with her family to Lubbock, Texas.

1931   Winnelle graduates from Lubbock High School. She meets future husband William Nelle while working at the family's boarding house in Lubbock.

1935   Winnelle graduates from Texas Tech University with a BA in home economics.

1935   June 22. Winnelle marries William H. Nelle at her family's home, the boarding house where they first met, in Lubbock, Texas. William is awarded an MA in Spanish from Texas Tech U., receives a fellowship to study at UC Berkeley.

1935   The Nelles move to Berkeley, California. Winnelle takes postgraduate courses in child psychology and public administration and is employed as a social worker in the Alameda County Welfare Department.

1945   William is awarded an MA in Spanish Literature from the University of California.

1946   May 18. Daughter Julia Annette Nelle is born in Berkeley, California.

1946	The Nelles move to Laramie, Wyoming. William becomes assistant professor and eventually head of the Department of Foreign Languages at the University of Wyoming while completing a PhD from the University of Nebraska. Winnelle pursues a career as a social worker and real estate property manager.
1974	William retires as professor emeritus from the University of Wyoming.
1977	Winnelle retires from her career in social work.
1983	The Nelles return to Lubbock, Texas.
1989	October 12. Winnelle Ward Nelle dies in Lubbock, Texas. Services at First United Methodist Church.
1998	July 6. William Nelle dies in Tacoma, Washington.

JULIAN E. WARD JR., MD

In 1958, Captain Julian E. Ward was deputy chief of the School of Space Medicine, Aviation Medicine Department at Randolph Air Force Base, San Antonio, Texas. He was then thirty-one years old, married and the father of three children—Sharon Ann, eight (b. 1950), Stuart Franklin, six (b. April 18, 1952), and Julian Elvis III, three and one half (b. 1954).

That same year, on April 1, he gave a public presentation, "Uncle Sam's First Space Men," to an audience at the Gunter Hotel in San Antonio, Texas, followed by a question-and-answer session. Here he showed that he belonged to the family tradition of "teacher," a role assumed by other Wards, including J. L. Ward, Julian's mother, and his older brother. Although still a young man, he was now a public figure, established as an authority in his chosen area of expertise: space medicine.

Figure 21. Julian E. Ward Jr., M.D.

In a 1958 North Carolina newspaper article, "Medical Men Say Space Flight Might Be Safer than Columbus,"[10] Captain Ward "described weightlessness as the biggest mystery in space medicine. Researchers have been able to duplicate the sensation for only thirty to forty seconds in airplanes. 'Investigations to date,' Ward said, 'have given no indication that medical problems arising from weightlessness will prevent manned space travel.'"[11]

"Weightlessness" might best be described as a state of freedom from the pull of Earth's gravitational field—freedom from the

10. *Greensboro Record*, May 1, 1958.

11. I remember him describing his own experience of weightlessness, achieved briefly in aircraft flying parabolic flight paths. He told of the way floating droplets of water released from a container would be attracted to and cover a person's face, giving them the sensation of drowning.

restrictions of gravity. Julian's research interest in weightlessness might then be seen as yet another example of the Ward family's search for freedom.

Julian's involvement in the space program should be seen in the context of the Cold War in which the United States was engaged following WWII, and in the context of President Kennedy's dramatic announcement of U.S. commitment to the goal of landing a man on the moon before the end of the 1960s. In the summary of Kennedy's speech below, note the goal's qualifier, "sending an American safely," a qualifier that precisely described the focus of Julian's work in the space program:

> On May 25, 1961, President John F. Kennedy announced before a special joint session of Congress the dramatic and ambitious goal of *sending an American safely* to the Moon before the end of the decade. A number of political factors affected Kennedy's decision and the timing of it. In general, Kennedy felt great pressure to have the United States "catch up to and overtake" the Soviet Union in the "space race." Four years after the Sputnik shock of 1957, the cosmonaut Yuri Gagarin had become the first human in space on April 12, 1961, greatly embarrassing the U.S. While Alan Shepard became the first American in space on May 5, he only flew on a short suborbital flight instead of orbiting the Earth, as Gagarin had done. In addition, the Bay of Pigs fiasco in mid-April put unquantifiable pressure on Kennedy. He wanted to announce a program that the U.S. had a strong chance at achieving before the Soviet Union. After consulting with Vice President Johnson, NASA Administrator James Webb, and other officials, he concluded that landing an American on the Moon would be a very challenging technological feat, but an area of space exploration in which the U.S. actually had a potential lead. Thus the cold war is the primary contextual lens through which many historians now view Kennedy's speech.[12]

---

12. Garber, "Decision." Emphasis added.

In August 1962, at the time of his death from a plane crash in Germany, Julian was preparing for reassignment back in the United States, to a new role at the Kennedy Space Center in Houston, to become more involved as a leader in the space medicine program there. He had nearly completed a tour of duty in Europe during which he organized a flight-based hospital unit that could respond quickly to a medical emergency anywhere in Western Europe.

Following the tradition of his Ward forebears, Julian explored the unknown as a scientist and pioneer, initially using Earthbound isolation chambers and short aircraft flights into the upper atmosphere to determine whether animals and then humans could travel safely in space. He wanted to instill confidence that those who might attempt space travel would be protected from its dangers, just as John Ward did for his family in the backcountry of America two hundred years earlier.

Prior to the experiments with humans, he monitored the health of animals (including mice and chimpanzees) in suborbital and orbital flights. He tracked the first manned space missions in Project Mercury from Tenerife in the Canary Islands, including the historic first U.S. orbital space mission of John Glenn in February 1962. He contributed to the design of the Mercury spacecraft used in Project Mercury.

The basic goals of Project Mercury were simple to state, more difficult to achieve: (1) Orbit a manned spacecraft around the Earth, (2) investigate man's ability to function in space, and (3) recover both man and spacecraft safely.[13]

Julian explored the possibility of human life in a condition of weightlessness, life beyond the limitations and restrictions of Earth. His goal was to achieve the ultimate freedom—to be free of Earth's gravitational pull, free of its atmosphere—freedom, ultimately, to undertake journeys into space, to explore the planets and stars, in safety. It was tragic and bitterly ironic that an Earthbound aircraft in which he was a passenger, on a routine flight just six months after Glenn's first Earth-orbital flight, plunged back to

13. Wade, "Mercury Mark 1."

Earth, taking Julian's life seven years before human beings would set foot on Earth's nearest planetary neighbor.

Julian Ward managed to author thirteen professional papers and coauthor two others on a diversity of scientific subjects in his short and busy lifetime. One publication that achieved widespread attention was "The True Nature of the Boiling of Body Fluids in Space," presented at a symposium on Medical Problems of Space Flight at the U.S. Air Force School of Aviation Medicine, January 19–20, 1956, published later that year in the *Journal of Aviation Medicine*.[14] It introduced the term "space ebullism": the vaporization of body fluids in space at body temperatures. As this and many other of his research publications show, Julian was fascinated by the challenge of human survival in the hostile environment in space or on other planets and the effects of freeing the body from the confines of Earth's gravity and atmospheric pressure.[15]

An excerpt from this paper is printed below. It summarizes the state of knowledge of the effect of weightlessness on blood pressure. As we have noted, weightlessness was a favorite topic of Julian's. Its exploration goes to the very heart of his scientific accomplishments. His pioneering work was essential, enabling extended space travel by human beings:

> Our present knowledge concerning the effects of the zero-gravity state upon circulation has been derived from brief periods of weightlessness in flight. However, from animal manned rocket studies by Henry and his associates, there is an indication that a fall in systolic and diastolic pressures may occur, possibly as a reaction of the cardiovascular system to short exposures to the gravity-free state. Actually hydrostatic pressures *per se* will not exist since the fluids are weightless; cardiac circulatory

14. J. Ward, "True Nature," 429–39.

15. His achievement was remembered in recent years by flight surgeon and astronaut Michael Barratt: "This is one of the landmark articles in the aerospace medical literature by one of our pioneers. Captain Ward was tragically lost in an aircraft accident. To honor his memory, the Society of US Air Force Flight Surgeons annually bestows the Julian Ward award for advances in aerospace medicine." Barratt, "Body."

pressures are basically tension pressures. The only effect of a constantly lower vascular pressure would be that intravascular vaporization will proceed much more violently and rapidly in free space than in a similar vacuum produced within an earthbound low pressure chamber. It is possible that on prolonged exposure to zero-gravity, compensatory mechanisms of vascular-pressor receptors will maintain relatively normal vascular tensions.

In a private letter to Julian's mother accompanying the establishment of the "Julian E. Ward Memorial Award" by his friends after Julian's death, Colonel Nuttall, president of the Society of USAF Surgeons, said,

> Major Ward will be long remembered as the finest and most outstanding flight surgeon of our time and the society is proud of the privilege and honor of sponsoring an award in Julian's memory. It is most fitting this is the only award which specifically recognizes specialty training in aviation medicine, since its theme and objectives are so representative of Julian's ideals and accomplishments. It will serve to stimulate all of the young physicians who select the specialty of aviation medicine.

Julian Ward, a gifted person of achievement, was also a charismatic personality, just as his parents, brother, sister, and other Wards had been, making loyal friends easily. A photograph of Julian lifting a live boa constrictor before a captivated group of Air Force servicemen is emblematic of this charisma. (The snake is an ancient symbol of protection, of life and healing.[16]) In much the same way, Julian, as a young child, had captivated residents at his mother's boarding house, and later, as a young father, performed magic tricks for his children, nieces, and nephews at family gatherings.

16. For instance, see Numbers 21:8-9.

Figure 22. Captain Ward charms his audience. The boa constrictor had been smuggled into the Air Force base from Panama.

JULIAN ELVIS WARD JR., MD'S TIMELINE

1927   March 15. Julian Elvis Ward Jr. is born in Wichita Falls, Texas.

1929   Julian moves to Lubbock, Texas with his family.

1944   June 16. Julian graduates from Berkeley High School, Berkeley, California and enters the University of California.

1945   April 28. Joins U.S. Merchant Marines, sees brief duty in the South Pacific.

1946   Julian enters the University of Texas.

1948	Graduates from the University of Texas with a BS in chemistry, cum laude.
1948	December 18. Julian marries Alma Augusta Kreider in the South Main Baptist Church and St. Ann's Roman Catholic Church, Houston, Texas.
1949	October 28. Daughter Sharon Ann Ward born in Houston.
1952	April 18. Son Stuart Franklin Ward born in Houston.
1952	Receives MD, MS (pathology, cum laude) degrees from Baylor College of Medicine. Completes internship at San Francisco City-County Hospital.
1953	Julian enters U.S. Air Force as first lieutenant. Helps develop a partial pressure suit (prototype space suit) at Gunter AFB, near Montgomery, Alabama, while serving as chief of the Flight Surgeon Section, School of Aviation Medicine, Gunter Branch. He begins his career in aviation and space medicine.
1954	August 13. Son Julian Elvis Ward III born in Montgomery, Alabama.
1955	Receives MPH degree (cum laude) from Harvard University School of Public Health.
1958	Julian named deputy chief, School of Space Medicine, Randolph AFB, San Antonio, Texas.
1958	July 29. National Aeronautics and Space Administration (NASA) created.
1958–59	Temporary assignment with NASA (California). Conducts experiments with mice in orbit. (Daughter remembers father's challenge transporting research animals aboard passenger aircraft.)
1959	Conducts Earth-bound isolation chamber experiments with human test subjects. Helps develop the Discoverer and Mercury Programs.

WHERE THE WATERS PART

1959–62   Major Julian E. Ward Jr., MD, USAF, commander

1959–62   Major Julian E. Ward Jr., MD, USAF, commander
           of the 49th Tactical Hospital at Spangdahlen AFB,
           Germany. During this assignment, he monitors
           the safety of manned space flights, including John
           Glenn's historic flight, from a telemetry station in
           the Canary Islands.

1962   August 13. Julian Elvis Ward Jr. dies at age thirty-
           five as a result of injuries from a plane crash in
           Germany.

1991   November 30. Alma Augusta Kreider dies in Aus-
           tin, Texas.

Epilogue

THE WARDS' SEARCH FOR freedom and authenticity involved finding a balance between them. It was not that freedom was necessarily inauthentic or that authenticity necessarily restricted freedom. Yet, at times, they were in conflict.

Freedom was expressed in both negative and positive senses: in the negative sense, it meant escape *from* barriers or restrictions (in sometimes thoughtless actions); in the positive sense, it meant finding a way *toward* new opportunities and experiences (in sometimes risky ventures).

Authenticity was expressed by remembering the themes and ideals valued over the generations by the Ward family, keeping them in mind as practical guides for living life. These themes and ideals were not so much "principles," left-brain-grasped lessons to be learned, as they were potent memories in the form of vividly recalled stories or mental pictures of events or episodes. As a rule (but not ordinarily stated *as a rule*), one should live one's life as a self-respecting, serious person of integrity, an engaged family member and citizen enjoying a good name in society, someone who is independent, self-sufficient, and doing the right thing (especially by explaining or guarding or investigating). One should

WHERE THE WATERS PART

have a healthy (but not *self-centered*) ego and seek opportunities to improve the material, social, and educational well-being of oneself and others. But one learned all this as if by osmosis, from hearing, repeatedly, the stories from the past.

Seeking authenticity ultimately meant true *self-fulfillment*: engagement of one's intelligence, talent, mental and physical strength; making good use of one's knowledge, education, or other resources to achieve those ends; and in so doing building social connections and establishing a good reputation. And it also meant not forgetting to look for fun and adventure along the way.

If these impulses got out of balance—if a desire for new experiences or the excitement of the moment took priority over living authentically, when the lure of a new adventure or escape from responsibility resulted in losing track of one's ideals—a life could go "off the rails" into self-centered egotism or risky behavior. The consequence might well be permanently damaged relationships with other people in the family or community. Such an imbalance unfortunately became evident in the lives of Abner V. Ward and James F. Ward Sr. One suspects it may also have happened in the lives of other high achievers in this family.

Health problems, including impulsiveness or other psychological problems, affected some of the Wards and their family relations. Revolutionary War veteran William Ward's mental disability, which manifested itself near the end of his long life, was declared to be "lunacy" by a court in Georgia—most likely an age-related dementia, a condition that today might be diagnosed as Alzheimer's disease. However, William could also have suffered from the effects of wartime trauma (PTSD or post-traumatic stress disorder) or suffered from disconnection with other family members. Julian Ward Sr.'s withdrawal to life at the boarding house (a sign of depression?) developed following his experiences as a travelling salesman during the Depression years.[1] And like William Ward, James F. Ward Sr.'s traumatic wartime experiences in the trenches of Iwo Jima are likely to have affected his psychological health.

---

1. Arthur Miller's *Death of a Salesman* (1949) captures some of these pressures at this time in America.

On the other hand, memories of the themes and ideals of this family were passed down and became the basis for the younger generations living lives of authenticity. The older family members, particularly the grandparents and uncles, influenced the younger family members. This influence was particularly notable as older siblings set examples for the younger. The influence of fathers on their children seems less clear. In at least one case there was conflict, such as that of Jacob's religious differences with William and his brothers. At the same time, William was strongly affected by his older brother John's enlistment in the Continental Army, getting married in a Baptist ceremony and moving a good distance away from his parents to live with like-minded neighbors in another state. William, just like his brother John, did all of those things, essentially following in John's footsteps (while at the same time being careful to not do them in just the same way, as that might conflict with his own decision-making or reputation for independence).

William is very likely to have grown up hearing the stories of his grandfather John's pioneering adventures after coming to America. In turn, William is likely to have influenced his grandson Lawrence with his own stories of the Revolutionary War, with its details of lengthy marches, hardships, camaraderie, glorious battles, and victories won—stories that were told at many family gatherings many years before L. L. made his own journey from Georgia to Texas.

Julian E. Ward Jr. was also strongly and undeniably influenced by his older brother Frank. Though he was a good fifteen years younger than Frank, Julian certainly did not want to miss wartime action in the South Pacific Theater (though that was limited to the last three months of World War II) or the respect he could gain from academic honors like those his brother had received, including the prestige of being awarded an MD degree. As in William Ward's case, Julian would certainly not want to follow his older brother's steps *too* closely (although, to be sure, he did find a way to get that Harvard degree!) Being authentic, for the Wards, meant first and foremost being true to yourself, not being imitative of another.

The importance of extended families and friends in shaping the ethical ideals is also clear. The legacy of the Scotch-Irish (who were mainly Presbyterians, including those Presbyterians who would eventually become Baptists) was to live in a serious, dedicated, morally upright community, to live a life accountable to God and to each other.[2] We saw this ideal at work in the community in the case of the immigrant Wards: James "the Elder," his sons James and John, John's grandson William and William's grandson, Lawrence, as well as William's great-grandson, Dr. Jesse Lawrence Ward. This ideal (or vestiges of it) may have appeared as a moralism, or fastidiousness towards policing others' morality.

Perhaps the most potent of the themes and ideals for these Wards was that of educational attainment, both of knowledge for its own sake and for the public respect and social opportunities enabled by it. We saw this ideal at work in the efforts of Franky Ward and her son L. L. Ward to ensure their respective children's early education, in J. L. Ward's dedication to expansion of higher educational opportunities in Texas, and in Julian E. Ward and Henrietta Ward's many sacrifices for their children's advanced educations. The ideal at work in these cases could be simply stated: all education is good and more education is better. The ideal was not simply attainment of education *per se* but education for the social prestige and influence over others to be gained from it, seen in the roles of teacher vs. student, lecturer vs. listener, or explainer of the mysteries of life vs. neophyte. The aim of education was essentially the aim of classical liberalism: freedom to pursue the life of the mind, freedom to pursue the True, the Good, and the Beautiful.

J. F. Ward Sr. searched for this ideal through reading literary classics and leading home discussion groups. The groups provided him opportunities to lecture to, and learn from, other dedicated learners. Underlying the ideal of education was the unquestioned

2. John Campbell expressed his family's ideals of living by the Golden Rule with their Irish neighbors, Catholic or Protestant; a sense of fairness in supporting religion; freedom of conscience to worship God in their own way; and bitterness toward the English landlords who treated their tenants unfairly; also, he expressed his father's opposition to slavery. Campbell, *Campbells*, 25, 41–43, 72.

belief that knowledge of the truth will set us free and that knowledge is empowering. Some of the Wards, at least, would add that knowledge is *spiritually* empowering, following the example of the Presbyterian Church, Baptist Church, or as that might also be said of Unitarianism and Freemasonry. Other family members would add that knowledge is *politically* empowering, following the example of liberalism or socialism. In all cases, in religion or politics, the ideal model for action was: first, become adequately informed of the issues; then, think independently and decide for yourself what's right and what's wrong; then, finally, move forward in confidence.[3]

What may best characterize this family from a survey of a 250-year span of one line of its ancestral history is its quest for freedom: freedom from oppression; freedom to think independently and make confident self-determinations of truth, goodness, and beauty; freedom to engage in adventures, especially adventures traveling to places of mystery; and the freedom to become an authentic person.

Success was not measured primarily by money or material "happiness" but by influence and reputation within the community, by *honestly* collecting "bragging rights" from the honors received and accomplishments realized. Honesty, or truthfulness, was highly valued and dishonesty, or lying, was abhorred.

What else can we conclude about this family? To speak in generalities, these Wards were (for the most part) friendly and well-liked, well-informed and quick-witted, ready to engage with or entertain others, ready to share their enthusiasm for almost anything, eager to draw the attention of others. They were curious about everything. They were hard-working, generous, and good citizens. They held high opinions of their own intelligence and abilities, opinions that were often—but perhaps not always—justified. Some of their acquaintances found this last characteristic irritating and off-putting. Others found it a positive experience being friends with a Ward, especially when learning new things in interesting or entertaining ways.

3. I remember Henrietta Ward's articulation of this formula.

The Wards were always teaching (or maybe lecturing), ready to expound upon favorite subjects such as politics, religion, history, art, or science. In some instances, they inspired devotion from others, which made them natural, charismatic leaders as salesmen, doctors, scientists, or ministers.

This family prized non-conformity and independence. Regardless of church or political affiliation, they were always separatists at heart, supportive of the American Revolution and of self-determination in politics and religion. Self-fulfillment continued to be an important ideal down to the last generation of Wards as they found their way into and out of the Baptist Church, into the professions, and into service organizations and social causes that valued humanism and Enlightenment ideals like science and education. This outlook led some to a conventional moralism and others to unconventional, eccentric behavior, vestiges of their heritage received particularly from the Scotch-Irish Presbyterians and the Baptists, a heritage of freedom to follow one's natural will as seen in the example given by Jonathan Edwards.

When the desire for freedom expressed in impulsive, self-centered thrill-seeking outweighed the desire for authenticity, a life could become unbalanced. Then real harm could be done to the individual and inflicted upon others, especially other family members. Fortunately, love and forbearance by the other family members could partially compensate for the disruption caused by these impulsive choices. And that love has benefited future generations, for which I (or we, that is, all their descendants) owe them the greatest debt of gratitude

Bibliography

Bailess, Shelley D. "Samuel Harris: Apostle of Virginia." *Journal of Backcountry Studies* 4/2 (2009) 1-10.

Barratt, Michael. "The Body at Vacuum." Episode 2691 of *The Engines of Our Ingenuity* (radio program), by John H. Lienhard, 2011. Transcript at https://www.uh.edu/engines/epi2691.htm.

Bates, Samuel P., and J. Fraise Richard. *History of Franklin County*. Chicago: Warner, Beers, 1887.

Bebbington, David W. *Baptists Through the Centuries: A History of a Global People*. Waco: Baylor University Press, 2010.

Bellah, Robert, et al. *Habits of the Heart: Individualism and Commitment in American Life*. Berkeley: University of California Press, 1985.

Bryan, Jimmy L., Jr. "The Patriot-Warrior Mystique." In *Texans and War: New Interpretations of the State's Military History*, edited by Alexander Mendoza and Charles David Grear, 113–32. College Station: Texas A&M University Press, 2012.

Campbell, John F. *The Campbells of Drumaboden*. Nashville: Foster & Parkes, 1925.

Cates, Cliff D. *Pioneer History of Wise County: From Red Men to Railroads— Twenty Years of Intrepid History*. Decatur, TX, 1907.

Chalkley, Lyman. *Chronicles of the Scotch-Irish Settlement in Virginia: Extracted from the Original Court Records of Augusta County, 1745–1800*. Vol. 2. Rosslyn, VA: Mary S. Lockwood and Commonwealth Printing, 1912.

Chepesiuk, Ron. *The Scotch-Irish: From the North of Ireland to the Making of America*. Jefferson, NC: McFarland, 2000.

Coldham, Peter Wilson. *The King's Passengers to Maryland and Virginia*. Westminster, MD: Family Line, 1997.

Collins, Travis. "Richard de la Warde (abt. 1040)." May 2019. https://www.wikitree.com/wiki/De_la_Warde-3.

Cooper, Roten. "John Ward (1606-1693)." September 2018. https://www.wikitree.com/wiki/Ward-3720.

"Culpeper Alexanders; Elk Run, Rapidan River, Border of Orange County, VA, 1764 Rent Rolls Culpeper Co., VA." February 15, 2013. https://www.ancestry.co.uk/boards/thread.aspx?m=4660&p=localities.northam.usa.states.virginia.counties.culpeper&dc=.

Dickson, R. J. *Ulster Emigration to Colonial America, 1718-1775*. Belfast: Ulster Historical Foundation, 2016.

Dorman, John Frederick. *Culpeper County, Virginia Deeds Volume One, 1749-1755*. Deed Book A and B. Washington: Dorman 1975.

———. *Culpeper County Virginia Deeds, Volume Two, 1757-1762*. Deed Book C. Washington: Dorman 1975.

Ebert, William Lawrence. "Captain Richard de la Warde." August 2019. https://www.geni.com/people/Captain-Richard-de-la-Warde/6000000012736237161.

Egle, William H., editor. *Notes and Queries: Historical, Biographical and Genealogical*. 3rd ser., vol. 2. Harrisburg, PA: Genealogical, 2015.

England, B. Jane. "Wise County." *Handbook of Texas Online*, June 15, 2010. https://tshaonline.org/handbook/online/articles/hcw14.

Federal Census, 1860, Western District, Upshur, TX.

Ford, Henry Jones. *The Scotch-Irish in America*. Princeton, NJ: Princeton University Press, 1915.

Garber, Steve. "The Decision to Go to the Moon: President John F. Kennedy's May 25, 1961 Speech before a Joint Session of Congress." NASA History, October 29, 2013. https://history.nasa.gov/moondec.html.

Hannah, Wayne, and Maureen Dorcy Hannah. "The People Called Scotch-Irish." In *A Hannah Family of West Virginia*, by Wayne Hannah and Maureen Dorcy Hannah. 9-11. Sheldon, WA, 2000. http://staff.washington.edu/jhannah/HannahBook/Ch02%20ScotchIrish.pdf.

Harrison, R. Ben. "Remembering a Revolutionary Hero." *Elberton Star*, March 9, 2005.

Havens, Paul Swain. *Chambersburg: Frontier Town, 1730-1794: A Bicentennial Narrative of the Origin and Growth of Chambersburg and Franklin County in Pennsylvania*. San Francisco: Craft, 1975.

Hill, Robert R. "Early Hills of the William-Hill-Susannah-Smither Line." October 1988. http://rancho.pancho.pagesperso-orange.fr/Hill.htm.

James, Linda. "Thomas Vernon (abt. 1686 – abt. 1756)." June 2019. https://www.wikitree.com/wiki/Vernon-326.

Kaminkow, Jack, and Marion Kaminkow. *A List of Emigrants from England to America, 1718-1759*. Baltimore: Magna Carta, 1984.

King, Alice B. "John Ward, Son of James the Elder." *Bulletin of the Watauga Association of Genealogists* 15 (1986) 56-60.

Lasher, George William, editor. *The Ministerial Directory of the Baptist Churches in the United States of America*. Oxford, Ontario: Ministerial Directory, 1899.

Mattox, Charles. "Heaven Is a Lot Like Kentucky: The Paint Creek Incident." *Bath County News-Outlook*, April 28, 2010.

McElwain, Wilbur J. *Genealogical Data Abstracted from History of Middle Spring Presbyterian Church, Middle Spring, Pennsylvania, 1738-1900*. Bowie, MD: Heritage, 1992.

"Medical Men Say Space Flight Might Be Safer than Columbus." *Greensboro Record*, May 1, 1958.

Melton, W. W. *Stories from Life*. Dallas: Helms, 1943.

Porterfield, Bill. "Brother Ward and 'Eighter from Decatur.'" *Dallas Times Herald*, June 1, 1983.

"Protest Against the Bill Establishing a Provision for the Teachers of the Christian Religion (November 2, 1785)." In "Legislative Petitions of the [Virginia] General Assembly, 1776-1865." http://www.virginiamemory.com/collections/petitions.

"Religion and the Founding of the American Republic: Religion and State Governments." Library of Congress exhibition. https://www.loc.gov/exhibits/religion/rel05.html.

Sacks, Oliver. *The River of Consciousness*. New York: Knopf, 2017.

Scott, Morgan. *History of the Separate Baptist Church: With a Narrative of Other Denominations*. Indianapolis: Hollenbeck, 1901.

"Sergeant William Ward." https://www.ancestry.com/family-tree/view/Military.aspx?tid=11354954&pid=678840622&vid=4ffae6af-a88d-4bb8-8f1d-9a4afd97bd79.

Stewart, Ezekiel. "Letter to Judge Michael Ward." 1729.

Taylor, Charles. *The Ethics of Authenticity*. Cambridge: Harvard University Press, 1992.

———. *Sources of the Self: The Making of the Modern Identity*. Cambridge, MA: Harvard University Press, 1989.

Tracy, James E. "Timber Ridge Presbyterian Church." Ch. 38 in *The Tracy Family History*. 2004. http://www.thetracyfamilyhistory.net/Ci_38_TRP_Church.htm.

Wade, Mark. "Mercury Mark 1." *Encyclopedia Astronautica*, 2019. http://www.astronautix.com/m/mercurymarki.html.

Ward, Andrew Henshaw. *Ward Family: Descendants of William Ward, Who Settled in Sudbury, Mass., in 1639*. Boston: S. G. Drake, 1851.

Ward, Cora. "The Ancient History of the Distinguished Surname Ward." November 2007. http://www.genealogy.com/forum/surnames/topics/ward/14802/.

Ward, Julian E. "The True Nature of the Boiling of Body Fluids in Space." *Journal of Aviation Medicine* 27/5 (1956) 429–39.

Ward, William. "Last Will and Testament." Georgia, Wills and Probate Records, 1742-1992. https://www.ancestry.com.

———. "Probate Records." Georgia, Wills and Probate Records, 1742-1992. https://www.ancestry.com.

Weekly Abstract of Sanitary Reports. Vol. 6. Washington, DC: Marine-Hospital Bureau, 1891. https://books.google.com/books?id=ZMAsAAAAYAAJ.

Williams, Michael E. *To God Be the Glory: The Centennial History of Dallas Baptist University: 1898-1998*. Arlington, TX: Legacy, 1998.